100 Leading Cases
in Law Enforcement

DATE D

Rolando V. del Carmen
Jeffery T. Walker

 anderson publishing co.
2035 reading road
cincinnati, ohio 45202
(513) 421-4142

Sam Houston State University

Briefs of 100 Leading Cases in Law Enforcement

ISBN 0-87084-090-8
Library of Congress Catalog Number 90-82312

Kelly Humble *Managing Editor*

Table of Contents

Table of Cases

PROBABLE CAUSE   1

DRAPER v. UNITED STATES
358 U.S. 307 (1959)

FACTS: A narcotics agent received information from an informant who had proven himself reliable that petitioner had gone to Chicago to bring three ounces of heroin back to Denver by train either the morning of September 8 or 9. The informant also gave a detailed physical description of petitioner, the clothes he would be wearing, and that he habitually "walked real fast." Based on this information, police officers set up surveillance of all trains coming from Chicago. The morning of September 8 produced no one fitting the informant's description. On the morning of September 9, officers observed an individual matching the exact description the informant had supplied get off of a train from Chicago and begin to walk quickly toward the exit. Officers overtook the suspect and arrested him. Heroin and a syringe were seized in a search incident to the arrest. The informant died prior to the trial and therefore was unable to testify. Draper was convicted of knowingly concealing and transporting drugs.

ISSUE: Can information provided by an informant, which is subsequently corroborated by an officer, provide probable cause for an arrest without a warrant? YES.

SUPREME COURT DECISION: Information received from an informant which is corroborated by an officer may be sufficient to provide probable cause for an arrest even though such information was hearsay and would not otherwise be admissible in a criminal trial.

REASON: The informant who provided information to the agent had provided reliable information in the past. When the agent personally verified each element of the informant's detailed description, except the part involving the possession of drugs, he developed probable cause to believe that the rest of the informant's description was true.

CASE SIGNIFICANCE: The evidence from the informant in this case could be considered hearsay, ordinarily inadmissible in a criminal trial. The Court said, however, that it could be used to show probable cause for purposes of a search; thus, evidence that may not be admissible in a trial may be used by the police to establish probable cause. This is important because all information from an informant is considered hearsay as the basis for police action, but the police can act on such information as long as it is good enough to establish probable cause. The Court held that there was probable cause here, because the information came from "one employed for that purpose and whose information had always been found accurate and reliable." The Court added that "it is clear that [the police officer] would have been derelict in his duties had he not pursued it."

RELATED CASES:
BECK v. OHIO, 379 U.S. 89 (1964)
ILLINOIS v. GATES, 462 U.S. 213 (1983)
McCRAY v. ILLINOIS, 386 U.S. 300 (1967)
UNITED STATES v. ORTIZ, 422 U.S. 891 (1975)

UNITED STATES v. CHADWICK
433 U.S. 1 (1977)

FACTS: Railroad officials in San Diego observed defendants who fit a "drug courier profile" (developed by the Drug Enforcement Administration) placing an unusually heavy footlocker which was leaking talcum powder (often used to mask the smell of marijuana) on a train. The officials notified federal narcotics agents who had officers waiting in Boston, the destination of the defendants. The officers in Boston did not obtained a search warrant but brought a dog trained to detect marijuana. The dog signaled the presence of marijuana just before the footlocker was lifted into the trunk of the defendant's car. Before the trunk's lid could be closed or the car started, police arrested the three suspects. A search incident to the arrest revealed no weapons, but the keys to the footlocker were taken from one of the suspects. Defendants and the footlocker were taken to the Federal Building. An hour and a half later, agents opened the footlocker without defendants' consent or a search warrant. Large amounts of marijuana were found in the footlocker. The defendants were charged with and convicted of possession of marijuana with intent to distribute.

ISSUE: May the police, with probable cause but without a warrant, search a movable container found in a public place? NO.

SUPREME COURT DECISION: The warrantless search of a movable container (in this case, a 200-pound footlocker secured by padlocks) found in a public place is invalid absent exigent circumstances.

REASON: "The factors which diminish the privacy aspects of an automobile do not apply to respondents' footlocker....Unlike an automobile, whose primary function is transportation, luggage is intended as a repository of personal effects...[and] a person's expectations of privacy in personal luggage are substantially greater than in an automobile....Nor does the footlocker's mobility justify dispensing with the added protections of the Warrant Clause.... [Finally] warrantless searches of luggage or other property seized at the time of an arrest cannot be justified as incident to that arrest either if the 'search is remote in time or place from the arrest,' or no exigency exists."

CASE SIGNIFICANCE: In ruling that the warrantless search of the footlocker was unjustified, the Court reaffirmed the general principle that closed packages and containers may not be searched without a warrant. The Court said that "unlike an automobile, whose primary function is transportation, luggage is intended as a repository of personal effects." A footlocker, by virtue of its being a repository of personal effects, injoys better protection and has greater expectations of privacy. The difference between the *Chadwick* case and the case of *United States v. Ross*, 456 U.S. 798 (1982) (where pieces of evidence obtained without warrant from a paper bag and a leather pouch were held admissible in court) is that *Chadwick* involved a footlocker, which was luggage and only incidentally loaded in a car when the seizure was made; whereas *Ross* involved a paper bag and a leather pouch, both of which were found in the trunk of the car and therefore could be opened without a warrant by the police.

RELATED CASES:
ARKANSAS v. SANDERS, 442 U.S. 753 (1979)
ILLINOIS v. ANDREAS, 463 U.S. 765 (1983)
NEW YORK v. BELTON, 453 U.S. 454 (1981)
TEXAS v. BROWN, 460 U.S. 730 (1983)

ILLINOIS v. GATES
462 U.S. 213 (1983)

FACTS: On May 3, 1978, the Police Department of Bloomingdale, Illinois, received an anonymous letter containing the following statements: that Gates and his wife were engaged in selling drugs; that the wife would drive her car to Florida on May 3 to be loaded with drugs; that Gates would fly down and drive the car back to Illinois; that the trunk would be loaded with drugs; and that Gates had more than $100,000 worth of drugs in his basement. Acting on the tip, a police officer obtained Gates's address and learned that he had made reservations for a May 5 flight to Florida. Arrangements for surveillance of the flight were made with an agent of the Drug Enforcement Administration. The surveillance disclosed that Gates took the flight, stayed overnight in a hotel room registered in his wife's name, and left the following morning with a woman in a car bearing an Illinois license plate, heading north. A search warrant for Gate's house and automobile was obtained on the basis of the officer's affidavit setting forth the foregoing facts and a copy of the anonymous letter. When Gates arrived at his home the police were waiting. A search of the house and car revealed marijuana and other contraband. Gates was charged with violating state drug laws and was convicted.

ISSUE: Did the affidavit and the anonymous letter provide sufficient facts to establish probable cause for the issuance of a warrant? YES.

SUPREME COURT DECISION: The two-pronged test established under *Aguilar* and *Spinelli* is abandoned in favor of a "totality of the circumstances" approach. The task of an issuing magistrate is to make a practical decision whether, given all the circumstances, there is a fair probability that the evidence of a crime will be found in a particular place.

REASON: "Unlike a totality-of-the-circumstances analysis, which permits a balanced assessment of the relative weights of all the various indicia of reliability (and unreliability) attending an informant's tip, the 'two-pronged test' has encouraged an excessively technical dissection of informants' tips, with undue attention being focused on isolated issues that cannot sensibly be divorced from the other facts presented to the magistrate."

CASE SIGNIFICANCE: The two-pronged test for establishing probable cause in cases in which information is given by an informant is now replaced with the "totality of circumstances" test, making it easier for police officers to establish probable cause for the issuance of a warrant. Under the two-pronged test as enunciated in *Aguilar v. Texas*, 378 U.S. 108 (1964), probable cause based on information obtained from an informant could be established only if the following were present: (1) reliability of the informant, and (2) reliability of informant's information. Both conditions must be satisfied before probable cause could be established. In contrast, under the "totality of the circumstances" test, probable cause may be established if, based on all the circumstances (including hearsay), there is a fair probability that contraband or evidence of crime will be found in a particular place. The *Gates* case still preserves the two-pronged test established in *Aguilar*, but it does not treat the two aspects separately and independently. Instead, the "totality of circumstances" approach is used, meaning that whatever deficiencies there may be in one prong can be supplemented or overcome by the other, together with other available evidence.

RELATED CASES:
AGUILAR v. TEXAS, 378 U.S. 108 (1964)
BRINEGAR v. UNITED STATES, 338 U.S. 160 (1949)
DRAPER v. UNITED STATES, 358 U.S. 307 (1959)
SPINELLI v. UNITED STATES, 393 U.S. 410 (1969)

UNITED STATES v. SOKOLOW
109 S. Ct. 1581 (1989)

FACTS: Sokolow purchased two round trip tickets for a flight from Honolulu to Miami under an assumed name. He paid for the tickets from a roll of $20 bills which appeared to contain about $4,000. He appeared nervous during the transaction. Neither he nor his companion checked their luggage. Additional investigation revealed that Sokolow had scheduled a return flight for three days later. Based on these facts which fit a "drug courier profile" developed by the Drug Enforcement Administration, officers stopped the pair and took them to the DEA office at the airport, where their luggage was examined by a narcotics-detecting dog. The examination indicated the presence of narcotics in one of Sokolow's bags. Sokolow was arrested and a search warrant obtained for the bag. No narcotics were found in the bag, but documents indicating involvement in drug trafficking were discovered. Upon a second search with the narcotics-detecting dog, narcotics were detected in another of Sokolow's bags. Sokolow was released until a search warrant could be obtained the next morning. A search of the bag revealed 1,063 grams of cocaine.

Sokolow was again arrested and charged with possession with intent to distribute cocaine. The U.S. District Court denied Sokolow's motion to suppress the evidence and he was convicted.

ISSUE: Were the factors matching Sokolow to a "drug courier profile" sufficient to justify his stop and subsequent search without a warrant? YES.

SUPREME COURT DECISION: Taken together, the circumstances in this case establish a reasonable suspicion that the suspect was transporting illegal drugs and therefore the investigative stop without warrant was valid under the Fourth Amendment.

REASON: Under the decisions in *Terry v. Ohio*, 392 U.S. 1 (1968) and *United States v. Cortez*, 449 U.S. 411 (1981), the totality-of-circumstances must be evaluated to determine probable cause for an investigative stop. Police officers may stop and briefly detain an individual in order to determine if they are involved in a criminal activity if the officer has reasonable suspicion supported by articulable facts that such activity is occurring.

CASE SIGNIFICANCE: This case addresses the issue of whether or not the use of "drug courier profiles" is valid under the Fourth Amendment. The Court said that there is nothing wrong with such use in this case because the facts, taken in totality, amounted to reasonable suspicion that criminal conduct was taking place. The Court indicated that whether or not the facts in this case fit a "profile" was less significant than the fact that, taken together, they establish a reasonable suspicion. In sum, the case appears to indicate that while a "drug courier profile" might be helpful, the totality of the circumstances is more important in establishing the legality of the stop and subsequent search.

RELATED CASES:
FLORIDA v. ROYER, 460 U.S. 491 (1983)
REID v. GEORGIA, 448 U.S. 438 (1980)
TERRY v. OHIO, 392 U.S. 1 (1968)
UNITED STATES v. CORTEZ, 449 U.S. 411 (1981)

THE EXCLUSIONARY RULE 2

WEEKS v. UNITED STATES
232 U.S. 383 (1914)

FACTS: Weeks was arrested for using the mail to transport tickets for a lottery. Other officers searched Weeks's home without a warrant and seized various articles and papers which were then turned over to the United States marshal. Later in the day, police officers returned with the Marshal and again searched Weeks's home without a warrant and seized letters and other articles. Weeks was charged with and convicted of unlawful use of the mail.

ISSUE: Is evidence illegally obtained by federal law enforcement officers admissible in court? NO.

SUPREME COURT DECISION: Evidence illegally seized by federal law enforcement officers is not admissible in federal criminal prosecutions.

REASON: The Fourth Amendment freedom from unreasonable searches and seizures applies "...to all invasions on the part of the government and its employees of the sanctity of a man's home and the privacies of life. It is not the breaking of his doors and the rummaging of his drawers that constitutes the essence of the offense; but it is the invasion of his indefeasible right of personal security, personal liberty and private property."

CASE SIGNIFICANCE: This decision excluded illegally obtained evidence from use in federal prosecutions. This rule was extended to state criminal prosecutions in 1961 in *Mapp v. Ohio*, 467 U.S. 643 (1961), making illegally obtained evidence inadmissible in both state and federal courts. It is interesting to note that from 1914 to 1960, federal courts admitted evidence of a federal crime if it was obtained illegally by state officers, as long as there was no connivance with federal officers. This questionable practice was known as the "silver platter doctrine." In 1960, the Court rejected the "silver platter doctrine," holding that the Fourth Amendment prohibited the use of illegally obtained evidence in federal prosecutions whether it was obtained by federal or state officers. *Elkins v. United States*, 364 U.S. 206 (1960).

RELATED CASES:
ELKINS v. UNITED STATES, 364 U.S. 206 (1960)
MAPP v. OHIO, 367 U.S. 643 (1961)
NIX v. WILLIAMS, 467 U.S. 431 (1984)
UNITED STATES v. LEON, 468 U.S. 897 (1984)

ROCHIN v. CALIFORNIA
342 U.S. 165 (1952)

FACTS: Having information that Rochin was selling narcotics, police officers entered his home and forced their way into the bedroom. When asked about two capsules lying beside the bed, Rochin put them in his mouth. After an unsuccessful attempt to recover them by force, the officers took Rochin to the hospital where his stomach was pumped. Two capsules containing morphine were recovered. A motion to suppress this evidence was denied and Rochin was convicted in a California state court of possession of morphine.

ISSUE: Were the capsules recovered after pumping Rochin's stomach admissible as evidence in court? NO.

SUPREME COURT DECISION: Although searches by state law enforcement officers are not governed by the exclusionary rule, some searches are so "shocking to the conscience" as to require exclusion of the evidence seized based on the due process (fundamental fairness) clause of the Constitution. These cases are limited to acts of coercion, violence and brutality.

REASON: "...[T]he proceedings by which this conviction was obtained do more than offend some fastidious squeamishness or private sentimentalism about combatting crime too energetically. This is conduct that shocks the conscience. Illegally breaking into the privacy of the petitioner, the struggle to open his mouth and remove what was there, the forcible extraction of his stomach's contents -- this course of proceeding by agents of the government to obtain evidence is bound to offend even hardened sensibilities. They are methods too close to the rack and screw to permit of constitutional differentiation."

CASE SIGNIFICANCE: This case was decided prior to the extension of the exclusionary rule to the states in 1961. In this state prosecution, however, the Court decided that the evidence obtained could not be used in court, not because of the exclusionary rule but because the conduct of the police officers was shocking and therefore violated the suspect's right to due process guaranteed by the Fourteenth Amendment. If the case were to be decided today, the evidence would be excluded under the exclusionary rule, not under due process.

RELATED CASES:
ASHCRAFT v. TENNESSEE, 322 U.S. 143 (1944)
BROWN v. MISSISSIPPI, 297 U.S. 278 (1936)
CHAMBERS v. FLORIDA, 309 U.S. 227 (1940)
ESCOBEDO v. ILLINOIS, 378 U.S. 748 (1964)

MAPP v. OHIO
367 U.S. 643 (1961)

FACTS: Mapp was convicted of possession of lewd and lascivious books, pictures, and photographs in violation of Ohio law. Three Cleveland police officers went to Mapp's residence pursuant to information that a person was hiding out in her home who was wanted in connection with a recent bombing. The officers knocked on the door and demanded entrance but Mapp, telephoning her attorney, refused to admit them without a warrant. The officers again sought entrance three hours later after the arrival of more police. When Mapp did not respond, the officers broke open the door. Mapp's attorney arrived but was denied access to his client. Mapp demanded that she see the search warrant the police claimed to possess. When a paper supposed to be the warrant was held up by one of the officers, Mapp grabbed the paper and placed it in her bosom. A struggle ensued and the paper was recovered after Mapp was handcuffed for being belligerent. A search of the house produced a trunk which contained obscene materials. The materials were admitted into evidence at the trial and Mapp was convicted of possession of obscene materials.

ISSUE: Is evidence obtained in violation of the Fourth Amendment protection from unreasonable search and seizure admissible in state court criminal prosecutions? NO.

SUPREME COURT DECISION: The exclusionary rule, applicable in federal cases, that prohibits the use of evidence obtained as a result of unreasonable searches and seizures is also applicable to state criminal proceedings.

REASON: "Since the Fourth Amendment's right of privacy has been declared enforceable against the States through the Due Proces Clause of the

Fourteenth [Amendment], it is enforceable against them by the same sanction of exclusion as is used against the Federal Government. Were it otherwise, then just as without the *Weeks* rule the assurance against unreasonable searches and seizures would be 'a form of words,' valueless and undeserving of mention in a perpetual charter of inestimable human liberties, so too, without that rule the freedom from state invasions of privacy would be...ephemeral..."

CASE SIGNIFICANCE: The *Mapp* case is significant because the Court held that the exclusionary rule was thereafter to be applied to all states, thus forbidding both state and federal courts from accepting evidence obtained in violation of the constitutional protection against unreasonable search and seizure. In the mind of the Court, the facts in *Mapp* illustrate what can happen if police conduct is not restricted. *Mapp* was therefore an ideal case for the Court to use in settling an issue that had to be addressed: whether the exclusionary rule should be applicable to state criminal proceedings. The Court answered with a definite yes.

RELATED CASES:
BOYD v. UNITED STATES, 116 U.S. 616 (1886)
ELKINS v. UNITED STATES, 364 U.S. 206 (1960)
ROCHIN v. CALIFORNIA, 342 U.S. 165 (1952)
WEEKS v. UNITED STATES, 232 U.S. 383 (1914)

UNITED STATES v. CREWS
445 U.S. 463 (1980)

FACTS: Immediately after being assaulted and robbed at gunpoint, the victim notified the police and gave them a full description of her assailant. Several days later, a man matching the description was seen by police near the scene of the crime. After an attempt to photograph him failed, he was taken to the police station, questioned briefly, photographed, and released. The victim identified the photograph as that of her assailant. Crews was then taken into custody and identified by the victim in a lineup. On a pretrial motion to suppress, the court ruled that the initial detention constituted an arrest without probable cause and that the photographs and lineup identifications were not admissible. The court, however, ruled that the courtroom identification by the victim was admissible. Crews was convicted of armed robbery.

ISSUE: Is an in-court identification that is the result of an illegal initial arrest admissible as evidence in court?

SUPREME COURT DECISION: The pretrial identification of the suspect in a photograph and lineup are not admissible as evidence due to the illegal arrest. The in-court identification, however, is admissible because the victim's recollections were independent of the police misconduct.

REASON: The courtroom identification by the victim was wholly independent of any police misconduct. Aside from the fact that Crews was present in the courtroom, partially as the result of the illegal arrest, the prosecutor's case was established from the courtroom identification by the victim which had nothing to do with the arrest. The conviction, independently established, was legal.

CASE SIGNIFICANCE: This case introduced the doctrine of "independent untainted source," an exception to the exclusionary rule. Under this exception, the police may use evidence related to an illegal search as long as it is not connected to the illegality. The Court said that the initial illegality (in this case the illegal detention of the suspect) could not deprive prosecutors of the opportunity to prove the defendant's guilt through the introduction of evidence wholly untainted by police misconduct. For example, a 14-year-old girl was found in the defendant's apartment during an illegal search. The girl's testimony that the defendant had sex with her was admissible because she was an independent source that predated the search of the apartment. Prior to the search, the girl's parents had reported her missing, and a police informant had already located her in the defendant's apartment. *State v. O'Bremski*, 70 Wash. 2d 425 (1967). Note, however, that if the evidence has been tainted by police misconduct, such evidence cannot be admitted in court. *Wong Sun v. United States*, 371 U.S. 471 (1963)

RELATED CASES:
WONG SUN v. UNITED STATES, 371 U.S. 471 (1963)
TAYLOR v. ALABAMA, 457 U.S. 687 (1982)
FRISBIE v. COLLINS, 342 U.S. 519 (1952)
WEEKS v. UNITED STATES, 232 U.S. 383 (1914)

NIX v. WILLIAMS
467 U.S. 431 (1984)

FACTS: On December 24 a ten-year-old girl disappeared from a YMCA building in Des Moines, Iowa. A short time later, Williams was seen leaving the YMCA with a large bundle wrapped in a blanket. A 14-year-old boy who helped him reported that he had seen "two legs in it and they were skinny and white." Williams's car was found the next day, 160 miles east of Des Moines. Items of clothing belonging to the missing child and a blanket like the one used to wrap the bundle were found at a rest stop between the YMCA in Des Moines and where the car was found. Assuming that the girl's body could be found between the YMCA and the car, a massive search was conducted. Meanwhile, Williams was arrested by police in a town near where the car was found and was arraigned. Williams's counsel was informed that Williams would be returned to Des Moines without being interrogated. During the trip an officer began a conversation with Williams in which he said the girl should be given a Christian burial before a snowstorm which might prevent the body from being found. As Williams and the officer neared the town where the body was hidden, Williams agreed to take the officer to the child's body. The body was found about two miles from one of the search teams. At the trial, a motion to suppress the evidence was denied and Williams was convicted of first degree murder. The Iowa Supreme Court affirmed the conviction. Williams sought release on *habeas corpus* in U.S. District Court. That court ruled that the evidence had been wrongly admitted at Williams' trial. The Court of Appeals and the Supreme Court agreed. At his second trial, the prosecutor did not offer Williams's statements into evidence and did not seek to show that Williams had led the police to the body. The trial court ruled that the State had proved that, if Williams had not led the police to the body, it would have been found by the searchers anyway. Williams was again convicted of murder.

ISSUE: Was the evidence (the body) admissible in court on the theory that the body would ultimately have been discovered anyway because of the on-going search? YES.

SUPREME COURT DECISION: Evidence which is illegally obtained may be admissible if the police can prove that they would have discovered the evidence anyway through lawful means.

REASON: "The independent source doctrine teaches us that the interest of society in deterring unlawful police conduct and the public interest in having juries receive all probative evidence of a crime are properly balanced by putting the police in the same, not a worse, position than they would have been in if no police error or misconduct had occurred."

CASE SIGNIFICANCE: This case illustrates the "inevitable discovery" exception to the exclusionary rule. This exception states that evidence that is the "fruit of the poisonous tree," meaning obtained indirectly as a result of illegal police behavior (such as the illegal discovery of a map that tells where contraband is hidden) is admissible if the police can prove that they would inevitably have discovered the evidence anyway by lawful means. In this case, no Miranda warnings were given to the suspect before he confessed; hence, the evidence obtained was excluded during the first trial. But, because the evidence would have been discovered anyway as a result of the continued search, the Court said that the evidence could be admitted.

RELATED CASES:
CHAPMAN v. CALIFORNIA, 386 U.S. 18 (1967)
MURPHY v. WATERFRONT COMMISSION, 378 U.S. 52 (1964)
SILVERTHORNE LUMBER CO. v. UNITED STATES,
    251 U.S. 385 (1920)
WONG SUN v. UNITED STATES, 371 U.S. 471 (1963)

UNITED STATES v. LEON
468 U.S. 897 (1984)

FACTS: Acting on the basis of information from a confidential informant, officers initiated a drug trafficking investigation. Based on an affidavit summarizing the police officer's observation, a search warrant was prepared. The warrant was reviewed by three Deputy District Attorneys issued by a state court judge. Ensuing searches produced large quantities of drugs. Leon was indicted on drug charges. Motions to suppress the evidence were granted in part because the affidavit was insufficient to establish probable cause. The court rejected the notion of good faith of the officer and acquitted the defendants.

ISSUE: Is evidence obtained as the result of a search conducted pursuant to warrant issued by a neutral and detached magistrate admissible in court if the warrant is ultimately found invalid through no fault of the police officer? YES.

SUPREME COURT DECISION: The Fourth Amendment's exclusionary rule allows the use of evidence obtained by officers acting in reasonable reliance on a search warrant issued by a neutral and detached magistrate that is ultimately found invalid.

REASON: "In the ordinary case, an officer cannot be expected to question the magistrate's probable cause determination or his judgment that the form of the warrant is technically sufficient. '[O]nce the warrant issues, there is literally nothing more the policeman can do in seeking to comply with the law.' Penalizing the officer for the magistrate's error, rather than his own, cannot logically contribute to the deterrence of Fourth Amendment violations."

CASE SIGNIFICANCE: This case, together with *Massachusetts v. Sheppard*, 468 U.S. 981 (1984), decided on the same day, are arguably the most important cases decided on the exclusionary rule since *Mapp v. Ohio*, 367 U.S. 643 (1961). They represent a significant, although narrow, exception to that doctrine. In these two cases, the Court said that there were objectively reasonable grounds for the officers' mistaken belief that the warrants authorized the searches. The officers took every step that could reasonably have been taken to ensure that the warrants were valid. The difference between the *Leon* and *Sheppard* cases is that in *Sheppard* the issue was improper use of a search warrant form (the form used was used in another district to search for controlled substances, the judge telling the detective who filed the form that the necessary changes would be made by the judge); whereas, in *Leon* the issue was the use of a questionable informant and stale information. The cases are similar, however in that the mistakes were made by judges, not the police. The Court said that the evidence in both cases was admissible because the judge, not the police, erred and theexclusionary rule is designed to control the conduct of the police, not the conduct of judges.

RELATED CASES:
AGUILAR v. TEXAS, 378 U.S. 108 (1964)
ILLINOIS v. KRULL, 480 U.S. 340 (1987).
MAPP v. OHIO, 367 U.S. 643 (1961)
MASSACHUSETTS v. SHEPPARD, 468 U.S. 981 (1984)

MURRAY v. UNITED STATES
487 U.S. 533 (1988)

FACTS: Suspecting illegal drug activities, federal agents followed Murray and several co-conspirators. At one point, Murray drove a truck and another person drove a camper into a warehouse. Twenty minutes later, when the two emerged from the warehouse, law enforcement agents could see a tractor trailer bearing a long, dark container. The truck and camper were later turned over to other drivers who were arrested and found in possession of marijuana.

Upon receiving this information, the law enforcement agents returned to the warehouse, without a warrant, and forced entry. The warehouse was unoccupied but the agents observed, in plain view, several burlap-wrapped bales containing marijuana. The law enforcement agents left the warehouse without disturbing the bales and did not reenter until they had a valid search warrant. In applying for the warrant, the agents did not mention the forced entry into the warehouse and did not rely on any information obtained during that search. After obtaining the warrant, law enforcement agents returned to the warehouse and seized numerous bales of marijuana and a notebook listing the destinations of the bales. Murray was arrested for conspiracy to possess and distribute illegal drugs. His pretrial motion to suppress the evidence was denied and he was convicted.

ISSUE: Is evidence first observed in an illegal entry by officers but subsequently seized through a valid, independent, search warrant admissible in court? YES.

SUPREME COURT DECISION: Even if the police illegally enter private property, evidence initially discovered during that illegal entry may be admissible in court if it is later discovered during a valid search that is wholly unrelated to the illegal entry.

REASON: The Court reasoned that the evidence ought not to have been excluded just because of unrelated illegal conduct by the police. If probable cause for a search warrant can be established apart from any illegal activity by the police, the evidence obtained in the subsequent search should be admissible.

CASE SIGNIFICANCE: This case illustrates the "independent source" exception to the exclusionary rule. In this case, the police illegally entered the warehouse and discovered bales of marijuana. The Court said that the marijuana would be admissible nonetheless if the officers later searched the warehouse pursuant to a valid warrant that was issued based on information that was not obtained during the illegal entry. Therefore, an initial illegal entry does not automatically exclude the evidence if the evidence is not seized at that time but a valid warrant is later obtained without relying on information obtained during the illegal entry.

RELATED CASES:
NIX v. WILLIAMS, 476 U.S. 431 (1984)
SEGURA v. UNITED STATES, 468 U.S. 796 (1984)
SILVERTHORNE LUMBER COMPANY v. UNITED STATES,
    251 U.S. 385 (1920)
WONG SUN v. UNITED STATES, 371 U.S. 471 (1963)

STOP AND FRISK

3

TERRY v. OHIO
392 U.S. 1 (1968)

FACTS: A plainclothes officer with 39 years of experience, 35 years of which were as a detective and 30 years of which were in the same patrol area, observed two men standing on a street corner. It appeared that the two men were "casing" a store because each walked up and down, peering into the store window, and then both returned to the corner to confer. At one point the two men were joined by a third man, who talked to them and then left swiftly. After the officer observed the two rejoining the same third man a couple of blocks away, he approached them, identified himself, and asked for identification. Receiving a mumbled response, the officer patted down the outside clothing of the men. The officer retrieved a weapon from Terry and one other man. Terry and the other man carrying a pistol were charged with and convicted of carrying concealed weapons.

ISSUE: Is "stop and frisk" valid under the Fourth Amendment? YES.

SUPREME COURT DECISION: The police have the authority to detain a person for questioning even without probable cause to believe that the person has committed a crime. Such an investigatory stop does not constitute an arrest and is permissible when prompted by both the observation of unusual conduct leading to a reasonable suspicion that criminal activity may be afoot and the ability to point to specific and articulable facts to justify the suspicion. Subsequently, an officer may frisk a person if the officer reasonably suspects that he or she is in danger.

REASON: "...[T]he police should be allowed to 'stop' a person and detain him briefly for questioning upon suspicion that he may be connected with criminal activity. Upon suspicion that the person may be armed, the police should have the power to 'frisk' him for weapons. If the 'stop' and the 'frisk' give rise to probable cause to believe that the suspect has committed a crime, then the police should be empowered to make a formal 'arrest,' and a full incident 'search' of the person. This scheme is justified in part upon the notion that a 'stop' and a 'frisk' amount to a mere 'minor inconvenience and petty indignity,' which can properly be imposed upon the citizen in the interest of effective law enforcement on the basis of a police officer's suspicion." [footnotes omitted].

CASE SIGNIFICANCE: The *Terry* case made clear that the practice of stop and frisk is valid. Prior to *Terry*, police departments regularly used stop and frisk either by law or by judicial authorization, but its validity was doubtful because the practice was based on *reasonable suspicion* instead of probable cause, which was necessary in arrest and search cases. The Court held that stop and frisk is constitutionally permissible despite the lack of *probable cause* for either full arrest or full search, and despite the fact that a brief detention not amounting to full arrest is a "seizure" requiring some degree of protection under the Fourth Amendment.

RELATED CASES:
ADAMS v. WILLIAMS, 407 U.S. 143 (1972)
DUMBRA v. UNITED STATES, 268 U.S. 435 (1925)
HUSTY v. UNITED STATES, 282 U.S. 694 (1931)
UNITED STATES v. DIRE, 322 U.S. 581 (1948)

ADAMS v. WILLIAMS
407 U.S. 143 (1972)

FACTS: While patrolling a high-crime area of the city in the early hours of the morning, an officer was approached by an informant who had provided him with reliable information in the past. The informant told the officer that Adams, in a nearby car, was carrying narcotics and had a gun in his waistband. The officer proceeded to the car, tapped on the window, and asked Adams to open the door. When Adams rolled down the window instead, the officer reached inside the car and removed a revolver from the precise place the informant had said it would be (although it was not visible to the officer). Adams was arrested for unlawful possession of a weapon. A search incident to the arrest revealed more weapons and a quantity of heroin. Adams's motion to suppress the evidence was denied and he was convicted on a weapons and a narcotics charge.

ISSUE: May an officer make a "stop and frisk" under the doctrine set down in *Terry v. Ohio*, 392 U.S. 1 (1968), based on information provided by an informant? YES.

SUPREME COURT DECISION: Reasonable grounds for a stop and frisk do not rest solely on an officer's personal observations, rather they may be based on information provided by another individual.

REASON: "The Fourth Amendment does not require a policeman who lacks the precise level of information necessary for probable cause to arrest to simply shrug his shoulders and allow a crime to occur or a criminal to escape. On the contrary, *Terry* recognizes that it may be the essence of good police work to adopt an intermediate response."

CASE SIGNIFICANCE: This case settles the issue of whether or not information leading to a "stop and frisk" situation can come from an informant and not from direct police observation. It is clear that the police can make an arrest based on information from an informant as long as such information constitutes probable cause. It follows that if the police can make an arrest based on information from a third person (an informant), the police should also be able to effect a "stop and frisk" (a less intrusive act by the police) based on third party information -- as long as such information constitutes reasonable suspicion.

RELATED CASES:
DRAPER v. UNITED STATES, 358 U.S. 307 (1959)
DUMBRA v. UNITED STATES, 268 U.S. 435 (1925)
HUSTY v. UNITED STATES, 282 U.S. 694 (1931)
TERRY v. OHIO, 392 U.S. 1 (1968)

UNITED STATES v. HENSLEY
469 U.S. 221 (1985)

FACTS: Hensley was wanted for questioning about an armed robbery in St. Bernard, Ohio. The police issued a "wanted" flier to other police departments in the area. Knowing of the flier, and after inquiring without success as to the existence of an arrest warrant, officers in Covington, Kentucky stopped the automobile which Hensley was driving. Firearms were found in the car and Hensley was arrested. Hensley was ultimately convicted of being a convicted felon in possession of a handgun. He appealed the conviction, claiming that the stop was illegal because there was no probable cause and the evidence should thus have been excluded from admission in court.

ISSUE: May the police stop and briefly detain an individual who is the subject of a "wanted" flier from another jurisdiction? YES.

SUPREME COURT DECISION: When the police have a reasonable suspicion, grounded in specific and articulable facts (in this case the "wanted" flier), that an individual was involved in or is wanted in connection with a completed felony, a *Terry* stop may be made to investigate that suspicion.

REASON: "[W]here police have been unable to locate a person suspected of involvement in a past crime, the ability to briefly stop that person, ask questions, or check identification in the absence of probable cause promotes the strong government interest in solving crimes and bringing offenders to justice. Restraining police action until after probable cause is obtained would not only hinder the investigation, but might also enable the suspect to flee in the interim and remain at large....The law enforcement interests at stake in these circumstances outweigh the individual's interest to be free of a stop and detention that is no more extensive than permissible in the investigation of imminent or ongoing crimes."

CASE SIGNIFICANCE: *Terry v. Ohio*, 392 U.S. 1 (1968), the leading case on stop and frisk, has been applied primarily in instances when the police have reasonable suspicion that criminal activity may be afoot and when the suspect may be armed and dangerous. *Hensley* authorizes a *Terry*-type stop in cases in which the stop is based on the issuance of a "wanted" flier by a police department in another city and not on the possible commission of a criminal offense.   Moreover, the Court publicly recognized the need among law enforcement agencies for communication and cooperation, saying:

> In an era when criminal suspects are increasingly mobile and increasingly likely to flee across jurisdictional boundaries, this rule is a matter of common sense: it minimizes the volume of information concerning suspects that must be transmitted to other jurisdictions and enable police in one jurisdiction to act promptly in reliance on information from another jurisdiction.

RELATED CASES:
CARROLL v. UNITED STATES, 267 U.S. 132 (1925)
DUNAWAY v. NEW YORK, 442 U.S. 200 (1979)
TERRY v. OHIO, 392 U.S. 1 (1968)
UNITED STATES v. PLACE, 462 U.S. 696 (1983)

UNITED STATES v. SHARPE
407 U.S. 675 (1985)

FACTS: An agent of the U.S. Drug Enforcement Administration (DEA) was patrolling in an area under surveillance for suspected drug trafficking when he observed Sharpe's car driving in tandem with an apparently overloaded truck which was driven by Savage. After following the two vehicles for 20 miles, the agent radioed for a marked car to assist him in making an investigatory stop. The two officers followed the vehicles several more miles at speeds in excess of the speed limit. The DEA agent stopped the car driven by Sharpe, but the officer was forced to chase the truck, which he stopped a half-mile later.

The DEA agent radioed for additional uniformed officers to detain Sharpe while the situation was investigated. These officers arrived ten minutes later. The DEA agent arrived at the location of the truck approximately 15 minutes after it had been stopped. The agent's requests to search the truck were denied, but after he smelled marijuana, he took the keys from the ignition, opened the back of the truck, and found marijuana. Savage was then placed under arrest and the officers returned to arrest Sharpe approximately 40 minutes after his car had been stopped. Sharpe and Savage were charged with and convicted of possession of a controlled substance.

ISSUE: Can a suspect be detained for a period of 20 minutes while officers conduct a limited investigation of suspected criminal activity? YES.

SUPREME COURT DECISION: The detention of a driver for 20 minutes was considered reasonable in view of the circumstances surrounding this case. There is no rigid time limit for the length of an investigatory stop; instead, the following should be taken into account:
(1) the purpose of the stop;
(2) the reasonableness of the time used for the investigation that the offices want to conduct; and,
(3) the reasonableness of the means of investigation used by the officers.

REASON: "While it is clear that 'the brevity of the invasions of the individual's Fourth Amendment interests is an important factor in determining whether the seizure is so minimally intrusive as to be justifiable in reasonable suspicion,' we have emphasized the need to consider the law enforcement purposes to be served by the stop as well as the time reasonably needed to effectuate those purposes." [Citations omitted.]

"Clearly this case does not involve any delay unnecessary to the legitimate investigation of the law enforcement officers. Respondents presented no evidence that the officers were dilatory in their investigation. The delay in this case was attributable almost entirely to the evasive actions of Savage....."

CASE SIGNIFICANCE: This case answers the question, "How much time is allowed in cases of investigative stops?" The answer: there is no fixed time allowed; instead, it all depends upon the purpose to be served by the stop and the time reasonably needed to carry it out. In this case, the circumstances were such that the detention for 20 minutes was considered reasonable. The Court added that judges should refrain from second-guessing police officers' decisions, particularly when the police are faced with a swiftly developing situation, as was the case here. This means that the benefit of the doubt must be given to the police on questions of how much time is sufficient for an investigative stop. Police officers must be ready to justify the amount of time used for an investigative stop, based on the purpose of the stop and the investigative method used because an arbitrary delay would be considered unduly intrusive and unreasonable by the courts.

RELATED CASES:
FLORIDA v. ROYER, 460 U.S. 491 (1983)
MICHIGAN v. SUMMERS, 452 U.S. 692 (1981)
TERRY v. OHIO, 392 U.S. 1 (1968)
UNITED STATES v. PLACE, 462 U.S. 696 (1983)

ARREST 4

FRISBIE v. COLLINS
342 U.S. 519 (1952)

FACTS: Acting as his own lawyer, Collins brought a *habeas corpus* action in federal court seeking release from a Michigan state prison where he was serving a life sentence for murder. He alleged that, while he was living in Chicago, officers from Michigan forcibly handcuffed, blackjacked, and abducted him and took him back to Michigan. He claimed that the trial and conviction under such circumstances violated his due process rights under the Fourteenth Amendment and the Federal Kidnapping Act and were therefore void.

ISSUE: Does the unlawful arrest of a defendant affect the validity of the court's jurisdiction in a criminal proceeding? NO.

COURT DECISION: An unlawful arrest has no impact on a subsequent criminal prosecution. An invalid arrest, therefore, does not deprive the court of jurisdiction to try a criminal case.

REASON: "This Court has never departed from the rule announced in *Ker v. Illinois*, 119 U.S. 436, that the power of a court to try a person for crime is not impaired by the fact that he had been brought within the court's jurisdiction by reason of a 'forcible abduction.' No persuasive reasons are now presented to justify overruling this line of cases. They rest on sound basis that due process of law is satisfied when one present in court is convicted of crime after having been fairly apprised of the charges against him and after a fair trial in accordance with constitutional procedural safeguards. There is nothing in the Constitution that requires a court to permit a guilty person rightfully convicted to escape justice because he was brought to trial against his will."

CASE SIGNIFICANCE: The *Collins* decision constitutes what to some might be a surprising exception to the exclusionary rule. It would seem logical to think that if items subject to illegal search and seizure are not admissible in evidence, then defendants illegally arrested ought not to be subjected to court jurisdiction (for purposes of a trial) either. The Court disagrees, stating that "the power of the court to try a person for crime is not impaired by the fact that he had been brought within the court's jurisdiction by reason of a 'forcible abduction.'" It then added that "[t]here is nothing in the Constitution that requires a court to permit a guilty person rightfully convicted to escape justice because he was brought to trial against his will." Note that the *Collins* case was decided in 1952, before the exclusionary rule was applied to the states in *Mapp v. Ohio*. Nonetheless, the ruling is still valid today.

RELATED CASES:
EX PARTE JOHNSON, 167 U.S. 120 (1897)
KER v. ILLINOIS, 119 U.S. 436 (1886)
LASCELLES v. GEORGIA, 148 U.S. 537 (1893)
MAHON v. JUSTICE, 127 U.S. 700 (1888)

CUPP v. MURPHY
412 U.S. 291 (1973)

FACTS: Upon learning of his estranged wife's death, Murphy voluntarily went to the police station for questioning. After arriving at the station, where he was met by his lawyer, the police noticed a dark spot on Murphy's finger which they suspected might be dried blood from the murder. Murphy refused an officer's requests to take a sample of scrapings from his fingernails, placed his hands behind his back and in his pockets, and appeared to rub them to remove the spot. Under protest and without a warrant, the police took the fingernail samples. The samples were determined to have traces of skin, blood cells, and fabric from the victim's nightgown. Murphy was tried and convicted of second degree murder.

ISSUE: Does the taking of fingernail scrapings without consent or formal arrest violate the Fourth Amendment protection from unreasonable search and seizure? NO.

SUPREME COURT DECISION: The police may make a seizure without warrant of evidence that is likely to disappear before a warrant can be obtained. Given the facts of this case -- the existence of probable cause, limited intrusion caused by the station house detention, and the destructibility of the evidence -- the warrantless seizure by the police did not violate the right against unreasonable search and seizure.

REASON: "Where there is no formal arrest, as in the case before us, a person might [be]...less likely to take conspicuous, immediate steps to destroy incriminating evidence on his person." A full search of Murphy without formal arrest would have been unconstitutional under *Chimel v. California*, 395 U.S. 752 (1969); but the limited intrusion on Murphy was justified here because of probable cause.

CASE SIGNIFICANCE: This case illustrates the "evanescent evidence" exception to the warrant requirement. The general rule is that searches and seizures must be by virtue of a warrant. This rule, however, is subject to many exceptions. One of those exceptions is the "evanescent evidence" rule which means that the absence of a warrant does not invalidate the seizure if the evidence sought is likely to disappear unless immediately obtained. In this case, the blood on the suspect's fingernails could easily have been rubbed off by the suspect, and the evidence would have disappeared, had the police not acted immediately. The likelihood of disappearance of the evidence constituted an emergency that justified the warrantless seizure.

RELATED CASES:
CHIMEL v. CALIFORNIA, 395 U.S. 752 (1969)
DAVIS v. MISSISSIPPI, 394 U.S. 721 (1969)
SCHMERBER v. CALIFORNIA, 384 U.S. 757 (1966)
UNITED STATES v. DIONISIO, 410 U.S. 1 (1973)

DUNAWAY v. NEW YORK
442 U.S. 200 (1979)

FACTS: An informant implicated Dunaway in a murder but could not provide sufficient information to justify issuance of a warrant. The police, however, ordered Dunaway picked up and brought to the police station, where he was taken into custody. Although he was never told he was under arrest, there was evidence that "he would have been physically restrained if he had attempted to leave." At the station, Dunaway made statements implicating himself in the murder after receiving his *Miranda* warnings. Dunaway was charged with and convicted of murder.

ISSUE: May the police take any suspects into custody, transport them to a police station, and detain them there for interrogation without probable cause to make an arrest? NO.

SUPREME COURT DECISION: The taking of a person into custody against his or her will for the purpose of criminal prosecution or interrogation constitutes an arrest for which probable cause is needed. Therefore, probable cause is necessary for the stationhouse detention of a suspect when such detention is accompanied by interrogation (as opposed to just fingerprinting), even if no formal arrest is made.

REASON: "...[T]he detention of petitioner was in important respects indistinguishable from a traditional arrest. Petitioner was not questioned briefly where he was found. Instead, he was taken from a neighbor's home to a police car, transported to a police station, and placed in an interrogation room. He was never informed that he was 'free to go'; indeed, he would have been physically restrained if he had refused to accompany the officers or had tried to escape their custody."

"The central importance of the probable cause requirement to the protection of a citizen's privacy afforded by the Fourth Amendment guarantees cannot be compromised in this fashion....Hostility to seizures based on mere suspicion was a prime motivation for the adoption of the Fourth Amendment, and decisions immediately after its adoption affirmed that 'common rumor or report, suspicion, or even "strong reason to suspect" was not adequate to support a warrant for arrest.'"

CASE SIGNIFICANCE: This case resolves the issue of whether or not the stationhouse detention of a suspect, accompanied by interrogation, is so restrictive of a person's freedom as to be the equivalent of an arrest, which is illegal without probable cause. In this case, there was no probable cause to arrest the suspect, but there were reasons for the police to consider him a suspect in connection with a crime being investigated. The suspect was therefore asked to come to police headquarters. He was never told that he was under arrest, but probably would have been physically restrained had he attempted to leave. He received his *Miranda* warnings, was questioned, and ultimately confessed. The Court held that, since the suspect was in fact taken into custody by the police and not simply stopped on the street, probable cause was required to take him to the police station. Since probable cause was absent, suspect's detention at the stationhouse was illegal and the evidence obtained from him, despite the fact that the suspect was given the *Miranda* warnings, was inadmissible in court.

RELATED CASES:
BROWN v. ILLINOIS, 422 U.S. 590 (1975)
CUPP v. MURPHY, 412 U.S. 291 (1973)
DAVIS v. MISSISSIPPI, 394 U.S. 721 (1969)
MORALES v. NEW YORK, 396 U.S. 102 (1969)

PAYTON v. NEW YORK
445 U.S. 573 (1980)

FACTS: After two days of intensive investigation, police officers assembled sufficient evidence to establish probable cause to believe that Payton had murdered the manager of a gas station. Officers went to Payton's apartment to arrest him. They had no warrant although they had time to obtain one.

Although light and music emanated from the apartment, there was no response to their knock on the metal door. They summoned emergency assistance and used crowbars to break open the door and enter the apartment. There was no one in the apartment, but in plain view was a .30-caliber shell casing that was seized and later admitted into evidence at Payton's trial. Payton later surrendered to the police and was indicted for murder. In a motion to suppress the evidence, the court ruled that the search of the house was illegal and suppressed the evidence, but also said that the shell casing was in plain view and admitted it into evidence. Payton was ultimately convicted.

ISSUE: Does the Fourth Amendment guarantee against unreasonable search and seizure require officers to obtain a warrant if making a routine felony arrest when there is time to obtain a warrant?   YES.

SUPREME COURT DECISION: In the absence of exigent circumstances or consent, the police may not enter a private home to make a routine, warrantless felony arrest.   The evidence was not admissible because there was time to obtain a warrant and there were no exigent circumstances to justify a warrantless search.

REASON: "In terms that apply equally to seizures of property and to seizures of persons, the Fourth Amendment has drawn a firm line at the entrance to the house.   Absent exigent circumstances, that threshold may not reasonably be crossed without a warrant."

CASE SIGNIFICANCE: The *Payton* case settled the issue of whether or not the police can make a warrantless arrest in a routine felony case.   The practice was authorized by the State of New York and 23 other states at the time *Payton* was decided.   These authorizations are now unconstitutional and officers must obtain a warrant before making a routine felony arrest.   If the arrest is not routine (meaning exigent circumstances are present), a warrantless arrest can be made.

RELATED CASES:
CAMARA v. MUNICIPAL COURT, 387 U.S. 523 (1967)
JONES v. UNITED STATES, 357 U.S. 493 (1958)
TAYLOR v. UNITED STATES, 286 U.S. 1 (1932)
UNITED STATES v. SANTANA, 427 U.S. 38 (1976)

MICHIGAN DEPARTMENT OF STATE POLICE v. SITZ
__ S. Ct. __; 1990 WL 78597 (1990)

FACTS: The Michigan State Police Department established a highway checkpoint program pursuant to guidelines established by a Checkpoint Advisory Committee which governed checkpoint operations, site selection, and publicity. Under these guidelines, checkpoints would be set up at selected sites along state roads and all vehicles passing through the checkpoint would be stopped and the drivers checked for signs of intoxication. If intoxication was indicated, the vehicle would be pulled to the side of the road for further tests; all other drivers would be permitted to resume their journey.

During the only operation of the checkpoint, which lasted approximately 1 hour and 15 minutes, 126 vehicles were checked with an average delay of 25 seconds. Two individuals were arrested for driving under the influence of alcohol. On the day before the checkpoint was established, both respondents filed a suit in the county court seeking relief from subjection to the checkpoints.

ISSUE: Is the use of a sobriety checkpoint which stops all vehicles a violation of the Fourth and Fourteenth Amendments? NO.

SUPREME COURT DECISION: Sobriety checkpoints in which the police stop every vehicle do not violate the Fourth and Fourteenth Amendment protections against unreasonable searches and seizures and are therefore constitutional.

REASON: The Court said that sobriety checkpoints are a form of seizure, but such seizure is reasonable because the "measure of intrusion on motorists stopped briefly at sobriety checkpoints -- is slight." In *United States v. Martinez-Fuerte*, 428 U.S. 543 (1976), the Court used a balancing test to uphold checkpoints for detecting illegal aliens. The Court held that the state has a substantial interest in preventing illegal aliens from entering the United States. This substantial interest, when balanced against the degree of intrusion placed on motorists passing through the checkpoint, supported the constitutionality of the procedure under the Fourth Amendment. In this case, the Court decided that "[t]he intrusion resulting from the brief stop at the sobriety checkpoint is for constitutional purposes indistinguishable from the checkpoint stops we upheld in *Martinez-Fuerte*," hence the two cases were decided similarly by the Court.

CASE SIGNIFICANCE: For a long time, lower courts had conflicting opinions about the constitutionally of sobriety checkpoints. Courts in 21 states had upheld sobriety checkpoints, while courts in 12 states had declared them unconstitutional. By a 6-to-3 vote, the Court has now declared that the police may establish highway checkpoints in an effort to catch drunk drivers.

Although the Court admits that sobriety checkpoints constitute a form of seizure and therefore come under the Fourth Amendment, the intrusion on the driver is minimal and therefore considered reasonable, particularly in light of the state interest involved. The Court quoted media accounts of the seriousness of drunk drivers, saying "drunk drivers cause an annual death toll of over 25,000 and in the same span cause nearly one million personal injuries and more than five billion dollars in property damage." Balancing the state interest involved and the individual constitutional rights invoked, the Court came down on the side of the state, hence giving the police an added weapon in the fights against drunk drivers.

In an earlier decision, the Court said that police officers were not authorized to stop a single vehicle for the sole purpose of checking the driver's license and vehicle registration (*Delaware v. Prouse*, 440 U.S. 648 (1979)). In *Prouse*, the Court disapproved of random stops made by Delaware Highway Patrol officers in an effort to apprehend unlicensed drivers and unsafe vehicles because there was no empirical evidence to indicate that such stops would be an effective means of promoting roadway safety. In the *Sitz* case, however, the Court said that the detention of each of the 126 vehicles in Michigan resulted in the arrest of two drunk drivers, or approximately 1.5 percent of the drivers. This is a much higher percentage than the number of aliens (.12 percent) found in the *Martinez-Fuerte* case. The Court in *Sitz* decided in favor of the state for three reasons: (1) the balance of the state's interest in preventing drunk driving; (2) the extent to which sobriety checkpoints can reasonably be said to advance that state interest; and, (3) the minimal degree of intrusion upon individual motorists who are briefly stopped.

Police departments should note that the sobriety checkpoint procedures declared constitutional by the Court in *Sitz* were a product of careful study and thinking. According to the Court, the following were the main features of the Michigan procedure:

> ... checkpoints would be set up at selected sites along state roads. All vehicles passing through a checkpoint would be stopped and their drivers briefly examined for signs of intoxication. In cases where a checkpoint officer detected signs of intoxication, the motorist would be directed to a location out of the traffic flow where an officer would check the motorist's driver's license and car regis-

tration and, if warranted, conduct further sobriety tests. Should the field tests and the officers observations suggest that the driver was intoxicated, an arrest would be made. All other drivers would be permitted to resume their journey immediately.

The *Sitz* case does not allow police to make random stops; what it does authorize are well-conceived and carefully structured sobriety checkpoints such as that of Michigan.

Although sobriety checkpoints are constitutional, such may be prohibited by departmental policy or state law.

In a case decided less than a week after Sitz, the Court further strengthened the hand of the police in drunk driving cases when the Court ruled that the police may ask routine questions of suspected drunk drivers and videotape answers without giving the *Miranda* warnings. Ruling 8 to 1, the Court said that slurred answers in response to question about height, weight, and age are admissible in court to convict drivers despite the absence of *Miranda* warnings. *Pennsylvania v. Muniz*, __ U.S. __, __ S. Ct. __; 1990 WL 80461 (1990).

RELATED CASES:
BROWN v. TEXAS, 443 U.S. 47 (1979)
DELAWARE v. PROUSE, 440 U.S. 648 (1979)
UNITED STATES v. MARTINEZ-FUERTE, 428 U.S. 543 (1976)
UNITED STATES v. ORTIZ, 422 U.S. 89 (1975)

PENNSYLVANIA v. MUNIZ
__ S. Ct. __; 1990 WL 80461 (1990)

FACTS: An officer stopped Muniz's vehicle and directed him to perform three standard field tests. Muniz performed these tests poorly and informed the officer that he failed the tests because he had been drinking. The officer then arrested Muniz and took him into custody.

After informing him that his actions and voice would be videotaped, Muniz was processed through procedures for receiving persons suspected of driving while intoxicated. Without being given his *Miranda* warnings, he was asked seven questions regarding his name, address, height, weight, eye color, date of birth, and age. He was also asked, and was unable to give the date of his sixth birthday.

An officer directed Muniz to perform each of the sobriety tests he had performed during the initial stop, which he again completed poorly. While performing these tests, Muniz attempted to explain his difficulties in completing the tasks and often requested further instruction on the tests.

An officer then requested Muniz to submit to a Breathalyzer test and read him the law regarding sanctions for failing or refusing the test. After asking several questions and commenting on his state of inebriation, Muniz refused to submit to the test. At this point Muniz was read his *Miranda* warnings for the first time. He then waived his rights and admitted in further questioning that he had been driving while intoxicated. The evidence obtained by the police in the form of Muniz's responses and the videotape of Muniz's performance during booking was submitted into court over his objection and he was convicted of driving under the influence of alcohol.

ISSUE: Do the police need to give drunk driving suspects the *Miranda* warnings when asking routine questions and videotaping the proceeding? NO.

SUPREME COURT DECISION: The police may ask persons suspected of driving while intoxicated routine questions and videotape their responses without giving *Miranda* warnings. The questions and videotape do not elicit testimonial responses that are protected by the right against self-incrimination clause.

REASON: "The privilege against self-incrimination protects an 'accused from being compelled to testify against himself, or otherwise provide the state with evidence of a testimonial or communicative nature,' but not from being compelled by the state to produce 'real or physical evidence.' To be testimonial, the communication must, explicitly or implicitly, relate to a factual assertion or disclose information.

"Muniz's answers to direct questions are not rendered inadmissible by *Miranda* merely because the slurred nature of his speech was incriminating. Requiring a suspect to reveal the physical manner in which he articulates words, like requiring him to reveal the physical properties of the sound of his voice, by reading a transcript, does not, without more, compel him to provide a 'testimonial' response for the purposes of the privilege.

"However, Muniz's response to the sixth birthday question was incriminating not just because of his delivery, but because the content of his answer supported an inference that his mental state was confused. His response was testimonial because he was required to communicate an express or implied assertion of the fact or belief and, thus, was confronted with the 'trilemma' of trust, falsity, or silence, the historical abuse against which the privilege against self-incrimination was aimed."

CASE SIGNIFICANCE: This case aids the police in obtaining evidence for prosecutions in drunk driving cases. Another case, decided by the Court a few days earlier, holds that sobriety checkpoints in which the police stop every vehicle do not violate the Constitution, *Michigan Department of State Police v. Sitz*, __ S.Ct. __ ; 1990 WL 78597 (1990). Within a week's period, the Court gave the police a virtual one-two punch in DWI cases.

This case holds that the police may ask questions of a drunk driving suspect and videotape the whole proceeding without giving the suspect the *Miranda* warnings. This case, however, addresses only "routine" questions (namely: eye color, date of birth, and current age). Questions that are not routine were not addressed in this case. The fact that the answers to these seven questions were slurred and therefore incriminating did not render the evidence admissible.

Four justices who voted with the majority said that this decision constitutes a new exception to the *Miranda* rule, saying that this routine booking exception is justified because the questions asked are not intended to obtain information for investigatory purposes. Four other justices, however, said that the *Miranda* rule simply did not apply to such questions and therefore did not consider the ruling an exception to the *Miranda* rule. Despite this disagreement, the fact remains that, when asking routine questions, the *Miranda* warnings need not be given and that the videotaping of the proceedings is constitutional.

From the perspective of police officers, this case means that they now have greater leeway on handling DWI cases. From a legal perspective, however, the main issue is what kind of self-incriminating evidence is admissible in court. The rule is that the Fifth Amendment prohibition against self-incrimination (which is protected by the *Miranda* rule) prohibits only testimonial or communicative self-incrimination and does not prohibit physical self-incrimination. The asking of routine questions, the answers to which being slurred, and the videotaping of the proceedings were self-incriminatory, but such incrimination was physical; the *Miranda* warnings were, therefore, not needed and the evidence was admissible in court. Note, however, that Muniz's answer to the question about the date of his sixth birthday was excluded because "the content of his answer supported the inference that his mental state was confused." In sum, if the evidence obtained was *physical* instead of *mental* in nature, the evidence was admissible in court, even without the *Miranda* warnings being given.

RELATED CASES:
DOE v. UNITED STATES, 487 U.S. 201 (1988)
MIRANDA v. ARIZONA, 384 U.S. 436 (1966)
SCHMERBER v. CALIFORNIA, 384 U.S. 757 (1966)
UNITED STATES v. DIONISIO, 410 U.S. 1 (1973)

SEARCHES – IN GENERAL 5

ZURCHER v. STANFORD DAILY
436 U.S. 547 (1978)

FACTS: Responding to a call to quell a disturbance, police were attacked by a group of the demonstrators, resulting in several injuries to the officers. There were no police photographers in the vicinity of the attack. Two days later, a special edition of the student newspaper carried articles and photographs of the clash. The District Attorney's Office obtained a warrant to search the offices of the newspaper. The warrant affidavit contained no allegation that members of the newspaper staff were suspects in the disturbance. The search was conducted pursuant to the warrant and no locked rooms or drawers were opened. The search revealed only the photographs already published and no materials were removed from the paper's offices. Members of the staff filed suit seeking to have the court declare the issuance of the warrant illegal and unconstitutional.

ISSUE: Is it constitutional under the Fourth Amendment for a court to issue a warrant for the search of the premises of a third party when the police have probable cause to believe that fruits, instrumentalities, or evidence of a crime are on the premises but do not have probable cause to believe that the possessor of the property is involved in the crime? YES.

SUPREME COURT DECISION: Searches of property belonging to persons not suspected of crime are permissible as long as probable cause exists to believe that evidence of someone's guilt or other items subject to seizure will be found.

REASON: "A state is not prevented by the Fourth and Fourteenth Amendments from issuing a warrant to search for evidence simply because the owner or possessor of the place to be searched is not reasonably suspected of criminal involvement. The critical element in a reasonable search is not that the property owner is suspected of crime but that there is reasonable cause to believe that the 'things' to be searched for and seized are located on the property to which entry is sought."

CASE SIGNIFICANCE: This case is significant in that it expands the authority of the courts and the police to obtain warrants to search places or properties of third parties, meaning people who are not involved in the commission of a particular crime. Without this decision, it would have been difficult for the police to obtain evidence other than directly from the scene of the crime or from people nearby. This authority, however, cannot be used to conduct a "fishing expedition" for evidence in the home of a third person. The Court stressed that the search warrant can be issued only if there is probable cause to believe that evidence of someone's guilt or other items subject to seizure will be found.

RELATED CASES:
COUCH v. UNITED STATES, 409 U.S 322 (1973)
FISHER v. UNITED STATES, 425 U.S. 391 (1976)
SEE v. SEATTLE, 387 U.S. 541 (1967)
UNITED STATES v. KAHN, 415 U.S. 143 (1974)

STEAGALD v. UNITED STATES
451 U.S. 204 (1981)

FACTS: Acting on a warrant issued for a certain Lyons, Drug Enforcement Administration agents entered the home of Steagald to search for Lyons. The entry was made without a warrant. While searching the home of Steagald, the agents found cocaine and other incriminating evidence but did not find Lyons. Steagald was arrested and convicted on federal drug charges.

ISSUE: May an officer search for the subject of an arrest warrant in the home of a third person, absent exigent circumstances, without a search warrant? NO.

SUPREME COURT DECISION: An arrest warrant is valid for entry into a suspect's place of residence. It does not authorize entry into another person's residence. If the suspect is in another person's home, a search warrant is needed to gain entry into that home, unless there is consent or emergency circumstances that would justify a warrantless search.

REASON: "Two distinct interests were implicated by the search in this case -- Lyons' interest in being free from an unreasonable seizure and petitioner's [Steagald's] interest in being free from an unreasonable search of his home. Because the arrest warrant for Lyons addressed only the former interest, the search of petitioner's home was no more reasonable from petitioner's perspective than it would have been if conducted in the absence of any warrant." The search therefore violated the Fourth Amendment.

CASE SIGNIFICANCE: Having an arrest warrant does not authorize the police to enter a third person's home without a search warrant. This is because such entry violates the Fourth Amendment rights of the third person who may not be involved in the crime. This rule, however, is subject to two exceptions: "emergency circumstances" and consent of the third person. Emergency circumstances means that the police do not have to obtain a search warrant if circumstances are such that to obtain one would jeopardize the arrest. For example, if the police can establish that obtaining a warrant would allow the suspect to leave the premises and escape arrest, a warrantless arrest would be justified. Another example would be cases of hot pursuit. If a suspect being pursued by the police enters a third person's home, the police may enter the home without a warrant to capture the suspect. Consent of the third person makes the warrantless search valid as long as the consent is intelligent and voluntary.

RELATED CASES:
PAYTON v. NEW YORK, 445 U.S. 573 (1980)
WARDEN v. HAYDEN, 387 U.S. 294 (1967)
WELSH v. WISCONSIN, 466 U.S. 740 (1984)
ZURCHER v. STANFORD DAILY, 436 U.S. 547 (1978)

MARYLAND v. GARRISON
480 U.S. 79 (1987)

FACTS: Police officers obtained a warrant to search "the premises known as 2036 Park Avenue third floor apartment," for drugs and drug paraphernalia which supposedly belonged to a person named McWebb. The police reasonably believed that there was only one apartment at the location; in fact, there were actually two apartments on the third floor, one belonging to McWebb and one belonging to Garrison. Before the officers became aware that they were in Garrison's apartment instead of McWebb's, they discovered contraband that provided the basis for Garrison's conviction for violating a Controlled Substance Act.

ISSUE: Is a search of the wrong apartment valid if conducted pursuant to a search warrant issued on a reasonable but mistaken belief on the part of the officers that the address was correct? YES.

SUPREME COURT DECISION: The validity of a warrant must be judged in light of the information available to officers when the warrant is sought; thus, a warrant which is overbroad in describing the place to be searched based on a reasonable but mistaken belief of the officer is not in violation of the Fourth Amendment. In this case the search warrant was valid even though the warrant proved to be too broad to authorize the search of both apartments. Evidence obtained from the search may be used in a criminal trial.

REASON: "On the basis of the information that the officers disclosed, or had a duty to discover and to disclose, to the issuing magistrate, the warrant, insofar as it authorized a search that turned out to be ambiguous in scope, was valid when it [was] issued. The validity of the warrant must be judged in light of the information available to the officers at the time they obtained the warrant. The discovery of facts demonstrating that a valid warrant was unnecessarily broad does not retroactively invalidate the warrant."

CASE SIGNIFICANCE: One of the elements of a valid search is that the warrant must contain a "particular description of the place to be searched." This means that the warrant must remove any doubt or uncertainty about which premises are to be searched. The *Garrison* case appears to soften the demands of that requirement. Here was a case of mistaken place description, leading to a mistake in the execution of the warrant. Despite this mistake, which stemmed from a warrant that was characterized as "ambiguous in scope," the Court said that the "validity of the warrant must be judged in light of the information available to the officers at the time they obtained the warrant." The fact that later discovery found the warrant to be unnecessarily overbroad did not invalidate the warrant; neither did it affect the admissibility of evidence obtained. It is important to note that the Court found the warrant to be valid on its face although its broad scope led to an error in the place of execution. There was reasonable effort on the part of the officers to ascertain and identify the place that was the target of the search, nonetheless a mistake took place. This case should not be interpreted as validating all search warrants where there is a mistake made in the description of the place to be searched. The test as to the validity of search warrants which are "ambiguous in scope" appears to be "whether the officers' failure to realize the overbreadth of the warrant was objectively understandable and reasonable...."

RELATED CASES:
DALIA v. UNITED STATES, 441 U.S. 238 (1979)
GO-BART IMPORTING CO. v. UNITED STATES, 282 U.S. 344 (1931)

HILL v. CALIFORNIA, 401 U.S. 797 (1971)
MARRON v. UNITED STATES, 275 U.S. 192 (1927)

CALIFORNIA v. GREENWOOD
486 U.S. 35 (1988)

FACTS: Upon receiving information that Greenwood was engaged in narcotics trafficking, police set up surveillance of his home. Officers observed several vehicles make brief stops at the house during late-night and early morning hours, one of which was followed to another residence suspected of trafficking in narcotics. Officers then asked the trash collector to pick up the trash bags Greenwood had left to be collected and turn them over to the police. Once in police possession, officers searched the trash bags and found items indicating narcotics use. Based on this information, the police obtained a search warrant for Greenwood's home. There police discovered quantities of cocaine and hashish. Greenwood and a co-conspirator were arrested and charged with felony narcotics charges. After receiving reports of continued narcotics trafficking, police once again seized Greenwood's garbage and again found evidence of narcotics use. This resulted in a second search of Greenwood's home, which revealed additional evidence of narcotics trafficking. Greenwood was arrested again and charged with additional narcotics charges.

ISSUE: Are warrantless searches of garbage left outside the curtilage of the home for regular collection valid under the Fourth Amendment? YES.

SUPREME COURT DECISION: The Fourth Amendment does not prohibit a warrantless search and seizure of trash left for collection in an area accessible to the public.

REASON: "The warrantless search and seizure of the garbage bags left at the Greenwood house would violate the Fourth Amendment only if respondents [Greenwood] manifested a subjective expectation of privacy in their garbage that society accepts as objectively reasonable....It may well be that respondents did not expect that the contents of their garbage bags would become known to the police or other members of the public. An expectation of privacy does not give rise to Fourth Amendment protection, however, unless society is prepared to accept that expectation as objectively reasonable....Here we conclude that respondents exposed their garbage to the public sufficiently to defeat their claim to Fourth Amendment protection. It is common knowledge that plastic garbage bags left on or at the side of a public street are readily accessible to animals, children, scavengers, snoops, and other members of the public...."

CASE SIGNIFICANCE: This case settles an issue that divided federal appellate courts, whether garbage left outside the curtilage of a home for collection is deemed abandoned such that it can be seized by the police without a warrant. The Court makes it clear that garbage left in that condition no longer enjoys the protection of the Constitution and therefore may be seized without a warrant. The test used was whether the original owner of the trash nonetheless enjoyed a "reasonable expectation of privacy" despite its being left outside the curtilage. The Court answered no, saying that "having deposited their garbage 'in an area particularly suited for public inspection and in a manner of speaking, public consumption, for the express purpose of having strangers take it,' respondents could have no reasonable expectation of privacy in the inculpatory items that they discarded." [Citations omitted.] The case therefore allows officers to delve into a person's garbage left at the curb so as to gather evidence of criminality without a warrant. It is logical to assume that newspaper reporters and other individuals may also do so without violating the original owner's property rights.

RELATED CASES:
ABEL v. UNITED STATES, 362 U.S. 217 (1960)
ESTER v. UNITED STATES, 265 U.S. 57 (1924)
KATZ v. UNITED STATES, 389 U.S. 347 (1967)
UNITED STATES v. VAN LEEUWEN, 397 U.S. 249 (1970)

MICHIGAN v. CHESTERNUT
486 U.S. 567 (1988)

FACTS: Chesternut began to run after observing the approach of a police car. Officers followed him to "see where he was going." As the officers drove alongside Chesternut, they observed him pull a number of packets from his pocket and throw them away. The officers stopped and seized the packets, concluding that they might be contraband. Chesternut was then arrested. A subsequent search revealed more narcotics. Chesternut was charged with felony narcotics possession.

ISSUE: Did the officer's investigatory pursuit of Chesternut to "see where he was going" constitute a seizure under the Fourth Amendment? NO.

SUPREME COURT DECISION: The appropriate test to determine if a seizure has occurred is whether a reasonable man, viewing the police conduct and surrounding circumstances, would conclude that he is not free to leave. There is no seizure *per se* in police investigatory pursuits.

REASON: "No bright-line rule applicable to all investigatory pursuits can be fashioned. Rather, the appropriate test is whether a reasonable man, viewing the particular police conduct as a whole and within the setting of all the surrounding circumstances, would have concluded that the police had in some [manner] restrained his liberty so that he was not free to leave.... Under this test, respondent [Chesternut] was not 'seized' before he discarded the drug packets.... The record does not reflect that the police activated a siren or flashers; commanded respondent to halt or displayed any weapons; or operated the car aggressively to block his course or to control his direction or speed. Thus, respondent could not reasonably have believed that he was not free to disregard the police presence and go about his business. The police therefore were not required to have a particularized and objective basis for suspecting him of criminal activity, in order to pursue him."

CASE SIGNIFICANCE: This case provides guidelines to persistent and difficult question in police work: When is a person considered seized by the police? The question is important because seizure by the police involves the Fourth Amendment and sets in motion constitutional guarantees, particularly the requirements of probable cause and, whenever possible, a warrant. Absent seizure, the police do not have to abide by constitutional guarantees. The Court makes clear that there is no definitive test to determine seizure; rather, it sets the following guideline: "whether a reasonable man, viewing the particular police conduct as a whole and within the setting of all the surrounding circumstances, would have concluded that the police had in some way restrained his liberty so that he was not free to leave." The standard is not whether the police intend to make a seizure, but whether the suspect would have concluded (as a reasonable man would have) that the police had in some way restrained liberty so that he was to leave. This is ultimately a question of fact for the judge or jury to decide. Such determination, however, must be made by taking all surrounding circumstances into account, i.e., use of siren or flashers, commands to halt, etc. If the behavior of the police is passive rather than active, chances are that there is no seizure.

RELATED CASES:
INS v. DELGADO, 466 U.S. 210 (1984)
TERRY v. OHIO, 392 U.S. 1 (1968)
UNITED STATES v. KNOTTS, 460 U.S. 276 (1983)
UNITED STATES v. MENDENHALL, 446 U.S. 544 (1980)

BROWER v. COUNTY OF INYO
109 S. Ct. 1378 (1989)

FACTS: In an effort to stop Brower, who had stolen a car and eluded the police in a chase of over 20 miles, police placed an 18-wheeled truck across both lanes of a highway, behind a curve, with a police car's headlights pointed in a manner which would blind Brower. Brower was killed in the crash as a result of the roadblock. Brower's heirs and estate brought a civil rights (42 U.S.C. § 1983) action for damages against the police alleging a violation of Brower's constitutional right against unreasonable search and seizure.

ISSUE: Is a road block set up by the police to stop a fleeing suspect a form of seizure under the Fourth Amendment? YES.

SUPREME COURT DECISION: A seizure occurs when there is a "governmental termination of freedom of movement through means intentionally appied." Because Brower was stopped through means intentionally designed to stop him, the stop constituted a seizure.

REASON: "Consistent with the language, history, and judicial construction of the Fourth Amendment, a seizure occurs when governmental termination of a person's movement is effected through means intentionally applied. Because the complaint alleges that Brower was stopped by the instrumentality set in motion or put in place to stop him, it states a claim of Fourth Amendment 'seizure'."

CASE SIGNIFICANCE: The importance of this case lies in the Court's definition of a "seizure" under the Fourth Amendment. Decided in 1989, this case gives the latest and most authoritative guidance to police officers as to when "seizure" by the police takes place, particularly in the context of roadblocks. Under the Court's definition of seizure, a roadblock is a form of seizure; and, since the roadblock in this case was set up in such a manner that it was likely to kill Brower, the Court decided that there was possible civil liability for his death. The Court did not say, however, that the police were automatically liable. Instead, it remanded the case to the Court of Appeals to determine whether the District Court erred in concluding that the roadblock was reasonable. If the roadblock was reasonable, then no liability could be imposed on the police. If, however, the roadblock was unreasonable, liability could be imposed.

RELATED CASES:
CAMERON v. CITY OF PONTIAC, 813 F.2d 782 (6th Cir. 1985)
CONLEY v. GIBSON, 355 U.S. 41 (1957)
GALAS v. McKEE, 801 F.2d. 200 (6th Cir. 1986)
TENNESSEE v. GARNER, 471 U.S. 1 (1985)

SEIZURES – IN GENERAL 6

SCHMERBER v. CALIFORNIA
384 U.S. 757 (1966)

FACTS: Schmerber was arrested for driving under the influence of alcohol, which resulted in an automobile accident. After reading Schmerber his *Miranda* warnings, and while Schmerber was in a hospital being treated for injuries suffered in the accident, an officer directed a physician to draw a blood sample for purposes of chemical analysis. This was completed over the objection of Schmerber and against the advice of his counsel. Evidence of the chemical analysis, which indicated intoxication, was admitted in court over the objection of Schmerber and he was convicted.

ISSUE: Does the drawing of blood from a defendant over his or her objection violate the Fifth Amendment protection from self-incrimination or the Fourth Amendment protection from unreasonable searches and seizures? NO.

SUPREME COURT DECISION: The drawing of blood from a suspect without his or her consent to obtain evidence is not a violation of any constitutional rights as long as the removal is done by medical personnel using accepted medical methods.

REASON: "*Breithaupt* [*v. Abram*, 352 U.S. 432 (1957)] was also a case in which police officers caused blood to be drawn from the driver of an automobile involved in an accident, and which there was ample justification for the officer's conclusion that the driver was under the influence of alcohol. There, as here, the extraction was made by a physician in a simple, medically accepted manner in a hospital environment. There, however, the driver was unconscious at the time the blood was withdrawn and hence had no opportunity to object to the procedure. We affirmed the conviction there resulting from the use of the test in evidence, holding that under such circumstances the withdrawal did not offend "that 'sense of justice' of which we spoke in *Rochin v. California*, 342 U.S. 165." 352 U.S. at 435. *Breithaupt* thus requires the rejection of petitioner's due process argument and nothing in the circumstances of this case or in supervening events persuades us that this aspect of *Breithaupt* should be overruled."

CASE SIGNIFICANCE: The *Schmerber* case addressed and settled four constitutional issues suspects usually raised during pretrial identification: right against self-incrimination, right to counsel, right to due process, and right against unreasonable search and seizure. On the self-incrimination claim, the Court said that the seizure of "real or physical" evidence does not violate Fifth Amendment guarantees because the amendment applies only to testimonial evidence. This implies that a suspect cannot refuse to appear in a police line-up or show-up. The issue of right to counsel was dismissed by the Court, saying that there was no right to counsel at this stage. On the right to due process, the Court concluded that the extraction of blood in this case was valid because it was made by a doctor in a hospital and followed a medically accepted procedure. On the issue of unreasonable search and seizure (*Schmerber* alleging that the police could have obtained a warrant prior to blood removal), the Court ruled that the presence of exigent circumstances (the alcohol would be processed through the body and be lost in a short time) justified the warrantless seizure.

RELATED CASES:
BREITHAUPT v. ABRAM, 352 U.S. 432 (1957)
ROCHIN v. CALIFORNIA, 342 U.S. 165 (1952)
UNITED STATES v. DIONISIO, 410 U.S. 1 (1973)
WINSTON v. LEE, 470 U.S. 753 (1985)

WELSH v. WISCONSIN
466 U.S. 740 (1984)

FACTS: A witness saw Welsh's automobile being driven erratically, eventually swerving off the road and stopping in a field. Before the police could arrive, Welsh walked away from the accident. Upon arrival at the scene, the police were told that the driver was either drunk or very sick. The police checked the registration of the car and went to the owner's house without obtaining a warrant. The police gained entry to the house when Welsh's stepdaughter answered the door. Welsh was arrested and convicted for driving while under the influence of intoxicants.

ISSUE: Is a warrantless nighttime entry of a person's home to make an arrest for a nonjailable traffic offense constitutional under the Fourth Amendment? NO.

SUPREME COURT DECISION: The warrantless nighttime entry of a suspect's home to effect an arrest for a nonjailable offense is prohibited by the Fourth Amendment.

REASON: "Before government agents may invade the sanctity of the home, it must demonstrate exigent circumstances that overcome the presumption of unreasonableness that attaches to all warrantless home entries. An important factor to be considered when determining whether any exigency exists is the gravity of the underlying offense for which the arrest is being made. Moreover, although no exigency is created simply because there is probable cause to believe that a serious crime has been committed, application of the exigent circumstances exception in the context of home entry should rarely be sanctioned when there is probable cause that only a minor offense has been committed."

CASE SIGNIFICANCE: Probable cause and exigent circumstances almost always justify a warrantless search. This means that as long as probable cause and exigent (emergency) circumstances are present that justify immediate action by the officer, a warrantless search is valid. This case adds a third dimension to this general rule. Here the Court said that the gravity of the offense must be considered when determining whether or not a warrantless search can be undertaken. If the offense is minor and nonjailable, a warrantless entry into a home is not justified, particularly at night. There are, however, unanswered questions in this case. For example, what if the offense is minor but carries a jail term? Or, suppose the incident takes place during daytime? What is clear from this case is that a warrantless nighttime entry into a person's home to make an arrest for a nonjailable traffic offense is not valid under the Fourth Amendment.

RELATED CASES:
McDONALD v. UNITED STATES, 335 U.S. 451 (1948)
MICHIGAN v. CLIFFORD, 464 U.S. 287 (1984)
UNITED STATES v. CAMPBELL, 581 F. 2d 22 (2nd Cir., 1978)
UNITED STATES v. UNITED STATES DISTRICT COURT,
    407 U.S. 297 (1972)

WINSTON v. LEE
470 U.S. 753 (1985)

FACTS: In a shoot-out resulting from a robbery, a store owner was wounded in the legs and the assailant appeared to be wounded in the left side of the body. Some time later, officers responding to another call saw the suspect eight blocks from the store. He told the officers that he had been wounded when he himself was robbed. The suspect was taken to the same hospital as the store owner. While at the hospital, Lee was identified by the store owner as the man who had shot him. The state asked a court for an order directing Lee to undergo surgery to have the bullet removed. The doctors first said that there was some danger involved in the operation, but later testified that the bullet was lodged near the surface of the skin and could be easily removed with no danger. While Lee was being prepared for surgery it was discovered that the bullet was deeper than originally thought and would require surgery under general anesthesia with some risk involved. Lee then moved for a rehearing in the state court which was denied. The case eventually went to the United States Supreme Court.

ISSUE: May a state compel an individual to undergo surgery in a search for evidence of a crime? NO.

SUPREME COURT DECISION: Compelled surgical intrusions into an individual's body may be of such a magnitude that the intrusion is unreasonable even if it may produce evidence of a crime.

REASON: "A compelled surgical intrusion into an individual's body for evidence...implicates expectations of privacy and security of such magnitude that the intrusion may be 'unreasonable' even if likely to produce evidence of a crime.... The unreasonableness of surgical intrusions beneath the skin depends on a case-by-case approach, in which the individual's interests in privacy and security are weighed against society's interests in conducting the procedure. In a given case, the question whether the community's need for evidence outweighs the substantial privacy interest at stake is a delicate one admitting of few categorical answers."

CASE SIGNIFICANCE: This case is significant because it indicates that there are limits to what the government can do in an effort to solve a crime. Here the government sought a court order to recover a bullet lodged in the chest of a suspect. The evidence would have been conclusive against the suspect, but the Court held that not even a court of law could order that such surgery be performed because it would have been too intrusive into the suspect's body. In an earlier case (*Schmerber v. California*, 384 U.S. 757 1966)), the Court held that a state may, over the suspect's protest, have a physician extract blood without violating the suspect's rights. However, according to the *Schmerber* decision, the holding that the Constitution does not forbid minor intrusions into an individual's body under stringently limited conditions in no way indicates that it permits more substantial intrusions or intrusions under other conditions. The Court in *Lee* concluded that the procedure sought was an example of a "more substantial intrusion" cautioned against in *Schmerber* and, therefore, held that to permit the procedure would violate the suspect's right to be secure in his person, as guaranteed by the Fourth Amendment.ts

RELATED CASES:
BREITHAUPT v. ABRAM, 352 U.S. 432 (1957)
ROCHIN v. CALIFORNIA, 342 U.S. 165 (1952)
SCHMERBER v. CALIFORNIA, 384 U.S. 757 (1966)
UNITED STATES v. DIONISIO, 410 U.S. 1 (1973)

SEARCHES INCIDENT TO AN ARREST

7

WARDEN v. HAYDEN, 387 U.S. 294 (1967)
CHIMEL v. CALIFORNIA, 395 U.S. 752 (1969)
VALE v. LOUISIANA, 399 U.S. 30 (1970)
COOLIDGE v. NEW HAMPSHIRE, 403 U.S. 443 (1971)
UNITED STATES v. ROBINSON, 414 U.S. 218 (1973)
UNITED STATES v. EDWARDS, 415 U.S. 800 (1974)
MARYLAND v. BUIE, 58 LW 4281 (1990)
MICHIGAN v. SUMMERS, 452 U.S. 692 (1981)

WARDEN v. HAYDEN
387 U.S. 294 (1967)

FACTS: Police went to Hayden's house pursuant to a call from an individual who had followed a robbery suspect until he entered the house. Hayden's wife consented to a search of the house. Hayden was arrested when it was determined that he was the only man in the house. An officer, attracted to an adjoining bathroom by the sound of running water, found a shotgun and pistol in a flush tank. Another officer, looking for "a man or the money" found clothes fitting the description of those worn by the robber in a washing machine. All items of evidence were admitted at the trial. Hayden was convicted of armed robbery.

ISSUE:
(1) Was the search without a warrant valid; and,
(2) are items considered "mere evidence" (the pistol, shotgun, and clothes), as distinguished from contraband and instrumentalities of crimes, seizable by the police for use as evidence? YES.

SUPREME COURT DECISION:
(1) The warrantless seizure here was valid because probable cause and exigent circumstances were present.
(2) There is no difference between "mere evidence" and contraband or instrumentalities of a crime under the provisions of the Fourth Amendment. "Mere evidence" may be searched, seized, and admitted in court as evidence.

REASON: The search was valid because "[s]peed here was essential, and only a thorough search of the house for persons and weapons could have insured that Hayden was the only man present and that the police had control of all weapons which could be used against them or to effect an escape." "Nothing in the language of the Fourth Amendment supports the distinction between 'mere evidence' and instrumentalities, fruits of crime, or contraband."

CASE SIGNIFICANCE: This case establishes that a warrant is not needed if there is probable cause and "exigent" (emergency) circumstances. This justifies making warrantless searches and seizures. The Court also settled the issue whether or not "mere evidence" (as opposed to contraband or illegal items) can be seized by the police. Earlier cases decided by lower courts were divided on the issue. Under this ruling, any evidence, not just contraband, that can help prove the case against the defendant can be seized by the police.

RELATED CASES:
ANDRESEN v. MARYLAND, 427 U.S. 463 (1976)
McDONALD v. UNITED STATES, 335 U.S. 451 (1948)
STANFORD v. TEXAS, 379 U.S. 476 (1965)
UNITED STATES v. POLLER, 43 F.2d 911 (2d Cir. 1930)

CHIMEL v. CALIFORNIA
395 U.S. 752 (1969)

FACTS: Chimel was suspected of having robbed a coin shop. Armed with an arrest warrant (but without a search warrant), police officers went to Chimel's house and were admitted by his wife. Chimel was not at home but was immediately arrested when he arrived. The police asked Chimel if they could "look around." Chimel denied the request, but the officers searched the entire house anyway and discovered some stolen coins. At the trial, the coins were introduced as evidence over Chimel's objection. Chimel was convicted of robbery.

ISSUE: In the course of making a lawful arrest, may officers search the premises without a search warrant? YES.

SUPREME COURT DECISION: After making an arrest, the police may search the area within the person's immediate control. The purpose of such a search is to discover and remove weapons and to prevent the destruction of evidence.

REASON: "When an arrest is made, it is reasonable for the arresting officer to search the person arrested in order to remove any weapons that the latter might seek to use in order to resist arrest or effect his escape. Otherwise, the officer's safety might well be endangered, and the arrest itself frustrated. In addition, it is entirely reasonable for the arresting officer to search for and seize any evidence on the arrestee's person in order to prevent its conceal-ment or destruction. And the area into which an arrestee might reach in or-der to grab a weapon or evidentiary items must, of course, be governed by a like rule. ...There is ample justification, therefore, for a search of the ar-restee's person and the area within his immediate control."

CASE SIGNIFICANCE: *Chimel* categorically states that the police may search the area of the arrestee's "immediate control" when making a valid arrest, whether the arrest be with or without a warrant. That area of "immediate control" is defined by the Court as "the area from within which he might gain possession of a weapon or destructible evidence." *Chimel* therefore authoritatively settled an issue over which lower courts had given inconsistent and diverse rulings. The current rule is that the police may search without a warrant after a lawful arrest, but the extent of that search is limited to the area of the arrestee's "immediate control." The safest, and most limited, interpretation of the term "area of immediate control" is a person's wingspan where it might be possible to grab a weapon or destroy evidence. Some lower courts have given a more liberal interpretation to include such areas as the whole room in which the person is arrested. This interpretation appears to go beyond what the Court had in mind in *Chimel*.

RELATED CASES:
ABEL v. UNITED STATES, 362 U.S. 217 (1960)
KREMEN v. UNITED STATES, 353 U.S. 346 (1957)
VALE v. LOUISIANA, 399 U.S. 30 (1970)

VALE v. LOUISIANA
399 U.S. 30 (1970)

FACTS: After obtaining a search warrant, the police set up surveillance outside Vale's home. While watching the house they observed what they suspected to be an exchange of narcotics between Vale and a known addict. After the exchange of narcotics, the police blocked the path of the addict, arrested Vale on the front steps of his home, and searched the house. Narcotics were found in a bedroom. Vale was convicted of possession of heroin.

ISSUE: May the police make a warrantless search of a house incident to an arrest without exigent circumstances and in the absence of the arrestee? NO.

SUPREME COURT DECISION: The warrantless search of a house incident to an arrest when the arrest does not take place in the house is justified only in "a few specifically established and well-delineated exceptions." The facts here did not come under one of those exceptions.

REASON: "If a search of a house is to be upheld as incident to an arrest, that arrest must take place inside the house,..., not somewhere outside -- whether two blocks away, *James v. Louisiana*, 382 U.S. 36, 20 feet away, *Shipley v. California*, (395 U.S. 818), or on the sidewalk near the front steps."

CASE SIGNIFICANCE: The Court in this case gave a narrow interpretation to the phrase "area of immediate control" where a search incident to an arrest is valid. Here the arrest took place at the front steps of the house. The subsequent search of the house did not come under the area of allowable search and, therefore, the evidence obtained was not admissible in court.

RELATED CASES:
CHAPMAN v. UNITED STATES, 365 U.S. 610 (1961)
UNITED STATES v. JEFFERS, 342 U.S. 48 (1951)
WARDEN v. HAYDEN, 387 U.S. 294 (1967)
ZAP v. UNITED STATES, 328 U.S. 624 (1946)

COOLIDGE v. NEW HAMPSHIRE,
403 U.S. 443 (1971)

FACTS: A 14-year-old girl, left her home in response to a man's request for a babysitter. Thirteen days later her body was found by the side of a major highway. On January 28, the police questioned Coolidge in his home concerning the ownership of guns, and asked if he would take a lie detector test concerning his whereabouts on the night of the girl's disappearance. He produced three guns voluntarily and agreed to the lie detector test. The following Sunday, Coolidge was called to the police station to take the lie detector test and for further questioning. While he was being questioned, two officers (not those who had questioned him earlier) went to his house and questioned his wife. During the course of the questioning, she voluntarily produced four of Coolidge's guns and the clothes he was believed to have been wearing on the night of the girl's disappearance. After a meeting involving the officers working on the case and the Attorney General, the Attorney General signed an arrest warrant for Coolidge and search warrants for his house and car. Pursuant to those warrants, Coolidge was arrested and his cars impounded. The car was searched two days later and twice after that. Evidence presented over Coolidge's objection included gunpowder residue, microscopic particles taken from the car and from the clothes provided by Coolidge's wife, and a

.22 caliber rifle also provided by her. Coolidge was charged with and convicted of murder.

ISSUES:
(1) Was the warrant authorizing the search of Coolidge's house and car valid?
(2) If the warrant was not valid, could the seizure of the evidence in Coolidge's house and car be justified as an exception to the warrant requirement?
(3) Were the guns and clothes given to the officers by Coolidge's wife prior to the issuance of the warrant admissible as evidence?

SUPREME COURT DECISION:
(1) The warrant issued by the state's chief investigator and prosecutor (the state attorney general) was not issued by a neutral and detached magistrate; hence, the warrant was invalid.
(2) The evidence seized from Coolidge's house (vacuum sweepings of the clothes taken from the house) and from the car (particles of gunpowder) could not be admissible as exceptions to the warrant requirement.
(3) The guns and clothes given by Coolidge's wife to the police were given voluntarily; hence, they were admissible.

REASON:
(1) "When the right of privacy must reasonably yield to the right of search is, as a rule, to be decided by a judicial officer, not by a policeman or government enforcement agency." A warrant must, therefore, be issued by a neutral and detached magistrate.
(2) "Since the police knew of the presence of the automobile and planned all along to seize it, there was no "exigent circumstance" to justify their failure to obtain a warrant." Such warrantless seizures could not be justified under any of the exceptions to the warrant requirement.
(3) "[T]he policemen were surely acting normally and properly when they asked her [Coolidge's wife], as they had asked those questioned earlier in the investigation, including Coolidge himself, about any guns there might be in the house. The question concerning the clothes Coolidge had been wearing the night of the disappearance was logical and in no way coercive. Indeed, one might doubt the competence of the officers involved had they not asked exactly the questions they did ask. And surely when Mrs. Coolidge of her own accord produced the guns and clothes for inspection, rather than simply describing them, it was not incumbent on the police to stop her or avert their eyes."

CASE SIGNIFICANCE: The *Coolidge* case is best known for the principle that a warrant is valid only if issued by a *neutral and detached magistrate.* If issued by any person who has an interest in the outcome of the case (such as the state attorney general who was also the state's chief investigator and prosecutor in the case), the warrant is invalid. In this case, since the warrant was invalid, the state sought to justify the admission of the evidence under the various exceptions to the warrant requirement. The Court said that the evidence here did not come under such exceptions as "search incident to an arrest," "automobile exception," or the "instrumentality of the crime." The evidence (guns and clothes) given by Coolidge's wife, however, were admissible because they were given not as the result of improper conduct on the part of the police, but because she wanted to help clear her husband of the crime.

RELATED CASES:
CARROLL v. UNITED STATES, 267 U.S. 132 (1925)
CHIMEL v. CALIFORNIA, 395 U.S. 752 (1969)
SHADWICK v. CITY OF TAMPA, 407 U.S. 345 (1972)
WARDEN v. HAYDEN, 387 U.S. 294 (1967)

UNITED STATES v. ROBINSON
414 U.S. 218 (1973)

FACTS: Based on a previous investigation, a police officer stopped Robinson on suspicion that he was operating a motor vehicle after his license had been revoked. After making a full custody arrest with probable cause the officer made a search of Robinson's person. He felt an unrecognizable object in Robinson's left breast pocket but admitted in court that he knew it was not a weapon. The officer removed the object which turned out to be a "crumpled up cigarette package" that contained fourteen gelatin capsules of heroin. The capsules were admitted as evidence in Robinson's trial and he was convicted of possession of heroin.

ISSUE: Is it constitutional for a police officer to search (as opposed to merely frisking) a person's body after a lawful custodial arrest even though the officer does not fear for his or her personal safety or believe that evidence will be destroyed? YES.

SUPREME COURT DECISION: A body search is valid in any situation in which a full custody arrest occurs. There is no requirement that officers fear for their safety or believe that they will find evidence of a crime before the body search can be made.

REASON: "A custodial arrest of a suspect based on probable cause is a reasonable intrusion under the Fourth Amendment; that intrusion being lawful, a search incident to the arrest requires no additional justification. It is the fact of the lawful arrest which establishes the authority to search, and we hold that in the case of a lawful custodial arrest a full search of the person is not only an exception to the warrant requirement of the Fourth Amendment, but is also a 'reasonable' search under that Amendment."

CASE SIGNIFICANCE: *Robinson* allows the search of a person's body after a lawful arrest. Prior to *Robinson*, courts allowed a full body search (as opposed to a frisk) only if the officer feared for his or her personal safety. In this case, the officer had probable cause to make the arrest (therefore the arrest was valid), but admitted that he could not tell what the object was and did not feel there were reasons to fear for his safety. Under the then prevailing standard, the search would have been invalid. *Robinson*, therefore, expands the scope of search incident to a valid arrest and does away with the "fear for personal safety" limitation. It differs from *Chimel* in that the *Chimel* case deals with the "area within the arrestee's immediate control," whereas *Robinson* specifically refers to body searches. The suspect's body is obviously within the area of immediate control, but the authority to search it was not necessarily included in *Chimel* because a person's body enjoys greater protection from governmental intrusion than the area around the person.

RELATED CASES:
GUSTAFSON v. FLORIDA, 414 U.S. 260 (1973)
PETERS v. NEW YORK, 392 U.S. 41 (1968)
RAWLINGS v. KENTUCKY, 448 U.S. 98 (1980)
TERRY v. OHIO, 393 U.S. 1 (1968)

UNITED STATES v. EDWARDS
415 U.S. 800 (1974)

FACTS: Edwards was arrested shortly after 11 p.m., charged with attempting to break into a post office, and taken to jail. Subsequent investigation at the scene of the crime revealed that the attempted entry was made through a wooden window which had been forced open with a pry bar, leaving paint chips on the window sill. The next morning substitute clothes were purchased for Edwards and his clothes were seized and held as evidence. Examination of the clothes revealed paint chips matching those taken from the window. His motion to suppress the evidence seized from his clothes was denied and Edwards was convicted.

ISSUE: Is a warrantless seizure of clothes taken from a suspect several hours after being placed in custody valid under the Fourth Amendment? YES.

SUPREME COURT DECISION: After being lawfully arrested and placed in custody, any search conducted at the place of detention which would have been lawful at the time of the arrest may be conducted without a warrant even though a substantial period of time may have elapsed between the arrest and the search.

REASON: "This [search and seizure] was and is a normal incident of a custodial arrest, and a reasonable delay in effectuating it does not change the fact that Edwards was no more imposed upon than he could have been at the time and place of the arrest or immediately upon arrival at the place of detention."

CASE SIGNIFICANCE: A search incident to an arrest does not have to take place immediately after the arrest as long as such arrest is justified, as in this case. The key is whether or not the arrest was valid. If the arrest was valid and the suspect is in custody, the search may take place at a later time and the evidence will be admissible in court. There is reason to believe that the Court in this case would have considered the search as valid even if substitute clothing was available at the time Edwards was placed in custody.

RELATED CASES:
ABEL v. UNITED STATES, 362 U.S. 217 (1960)
COOPER v. CALIFORNIA, 386 U.S. 58 (1967)
GORIN v. UNITED STATES, 379 U.S. 971 (1965)
UNITED STATES v. ROBINSON, 414 U.S. 218 (1973)

MARYLAND v. BUIE
58 LW 4281 (1990)

FACTS: After surveillance, six or seven police officers obtained and executed arrest warrants for Buie and an accomplice in connection with an armed robbery. Upon reaching Buie's house, the officers "fanned out through the first and second floors." One of the officers observed the basement so no one would surprise the officers. This officer shouted into the basement and ordered anyone there to come out. A voice asked who was there. The officer ordered the person to come out three more times before Buie emerged from the basement. After placing Buie under arrest, another officer entered the basement to see if there was anyone else there. Once in the basement, the officer noticed in plain view a red running suit similar to the one worn by one of the suspects in the robbery. The running suit was admitted as evidence at Buie's trial over his objection, and he was convicted of robbery with a deadly weapon and using a handgun in the commission of a felony.

ISSUE: May officers conduct a warrantless protective sweep of the area in which a suspect is arrested in order to determine if another person might be there who would be a danger to the officers? YES.

SUPREME COURT DECISION: "The fourth Amendment permits a properly limited protective sweep in conjunction with an in-home arrest when the searching officer possesses a reasonable belief based on specific and articulable facts that the area to be swept harbors an individual posing a danger to those on the arrest scene."

REASON: "We...hold that as an incident to the arrest the officers could, as a precautionary matter and without probable cause or reasonable suspicion, look in closets and other spaces immediately adjoining the place of arrest from which an attack could be immediately launched. Beyond that, however, we hold that there must be articulable facts which, taken together with the rational inferences from those facts, would warrant a reasonably prudent officer in believing that the area to be swept harbors an individual posing a danger to those on the scene. This no more and no less was required in *Terry* and *Long* and, as in those cases, we think this balance is the proper one.

"We should emphasize that such a protective sweep, aimed at protecting the arresting officers, if justified by the circumstances, is nevertheless not a full search of the premises, but may extend only to cursory inspection of those spaces where a person may be found. The sweep lasts no longer than is necessary to dispel the reasonable suspicion of danger and in any event no longer than it takes to complete the arrest and depart the premises."

CASE SIGNIFICANCE: This case is significant because it authorizes the practice in some police departments of conducting a "protective sweep" during an arrest. It is important for police officers to note, however, that *Buie* does not give the police unlimited authority, when making an arrest, to search the whole house. The protective sweep allowed by *Buie* is limited in scope. The following limitations must be observed, taken from the language of the court's decision:

> (1) "There must be articulate facts which...would warrant a reasonably prudent officer tin believing that the area to be swept harbors an individual posing a danger;"
> (2) "Such a protective sweep is not a full search of the premises, but may extend only to a cursory inspection of those spaces where a person may be found;" and
> (3) The sweep lasts no longer than is necessary to dispel the reasonable suspicion of danger and in any event no longer than it takes to complete the arrest and depart the premises."

The police must be careful to observe the above limitations, otherwise the search becomes invalid.

Buie does not indicate a broadening of the Court's ruling in *Chimel v. California*, 395 U.S. 752 (1969), where the Court said that once a lawful arrest has been made, the police may search any area within the suspect's "immediate control."   The Court itself distinguished *Chimel* from *Buie* as follows:

> (1) "*Chimel* was concerned with a full-blown, top-to-bottom search of an entire house for evidence of the crime for which the arrest was made, not the more limited intrusion contemplated by a protective sweep; and
> (2) "The justification for the search incident to arrest in *Chimel* was the threat posed by the arrestee, not the safety threat posed by the house or more properly by unseen third parties in the house."

RELATED CASES:
ARIZONA v. HICKS, 480 U.S. 321 (1987)
CHIMEL v. CALIFORNIA, 395 U.S. 752 (1969)
MICHIGAN v. LONG, 463 U.S. 1032 (1983)
TERRY v. OHIO, 392 U.S. 1 (1968)

MICHIGAN v. SUMMERS
452 U.S. 692 (1981)

FACTS: While officers were executing a warrant to search a house for narcotics, they encountered Summers descending the front steps of the house. They requested his assistance in gaining entry to the house. He replied that he did not have keys to the front door but that he would ring someone over the intercom. Another occupant of the house answered the door but refused to admit the police. The officers gained entry to the house by forcing the door open. Officers detained Summers and eight others in the house while the premises were searched. When narcotics were found in the house, the police determined that Summers was, in fact, the owner of the house and arrested him. During a search of Summers incident to the arrest, officers discovered heroin in his coat pocket.

ISSUE: May the police detain a person on the premises while a search is conducted? YES.

SUPREME COURT DECISION: A warrant to search carries with it the limited authority to detain the occupants of the premises while the search is conducted.

REASON: "The detention of one of the residents while the premises were searched, although admittedly a significant restraint on his liberty, was surely less intrusive than the search itself. Indeed, we may safely assume that most citizens, unless they intend flight to avoid arrest, would elect to remain in order to observe the search of their possessions."

CASE SIGNIFICANCE: This case expands to a limited extent the search and seizure power of the police, enabling them to detain persons on the premises while a search is being conducted. A warrant to search for certain items may be used by the police to temporarily deprive a person found on the premises of liberty; such detention being merely a minimal intrusion of the person's Fourth Amendment right.

RELATED CASES:
DUNAWAY v. NEW YORK, 442 U.S. 200 (1979)
PAYTON v. NEW YORK, 445 U.S. 573 (1980)
UNITED STATES v. Di Re, 332 U.S. 581 (1948)
YBARRA v. ILLINOIS, 444 U.S. 85 (1979)

CONSENT SEARCHES 8

BUMPER v. NORTH CAROLINA
391 U.S. 543 (1968)

FACTS: During a rape investigation, and prior to his arrest, officers went to Bumper's home where he lived with his grandmother. One of the four officers went to the door and was met by the grandmother. When the officer announced that he had a warrant to search the house, the grandmother responded "Go ahead" and opened the door. The officers found a rifle in the kitchen which was seized and entered as evidence. Bumper was subsequently charged with and convicted of rape.

ISSUE: Can a search be justified as lawful on the basis of consent when that alleged consent is given only after the official conducting the search asserts possession of a warrant? NO.

SUPREME COURT DECISION: The alleged consent in this case was not voluntary because it was obtained by deception through a claim of lawful authority which did not exist. A search conducted by virtue of a warrant cannot later be justified by consent if the warrant turns out to be invalid.

REASON: "When a prosecutor seeks to rely upon consent to justify the lawfulness of a search, he has the burden of proving that the consent was, in fact, freely and voluntarily given. This burden cannot be discharged by showing no more that acquiescence to a claim of lawful authority. A search conducted in reliance upon a warrant cannot later be justified on the basis of consent if it turns out that the warrant was invalid....When a law officer claims authority to search a home under a warrant, he announces in effect that the occupant has no right to resist the search. The situation is instinct with coercion -- albeit colorably lawful coercion. Where there is coercion there cannot be consent."

CASE SIGNIFICANCE: Consent to search is not valid if permission is given as a result of police misrepresentation or deception. In this case, the police said they had a warrant when, in fact, they did not. Lower courts are divided on the related issue of whether consent is valid if the officer does not have a warrant but threatens to obtain one. That issue has not been resolved by the Supreme Court.

RELATED CASES:
AMOS v. UNITED STATES, 225 U.S. 313 (1921)
CHAPMAN v. UNITED STATES, 365 U.S. 610 (1961)

FRAZIER v. CUPP, 394 U.S. 731 (1969)
UNITED STATES v. MATLOCK, 415 U.S. 164 (1974)

SCHNECKLOTH v. BUSTAMONTE
412 U.S. 218 (1973)

FACTS: An officer on routine patrol stopped a vehicle containing Bustamonte and five others after observing that a headlight and the license plate light were burned out. When the driver could not produce a driver's license, the officer asked if any of the others had any type of identification. Only one, Joe Alcala, was able to produce a driver's license. He explained that the vehicle belonged to his brother. The men were ordered out of the car, and the officer asked Alcala if he could search the car. Alcala replied, "Sure, go ahead." Prior to the search, no one had been threatened with arrest or given the impression they were suspected of any wrongdoing. Alcala assisted in the search by opening the trunk and glove compartment. During the search, the officer found three checks under the left rear seat which had been stolen from a car wash. Using the checks as evidence, Bustamonte was convicted of possession of a check with intent to defraud.

ISSUE: Is knowledge by a suspect of the right to refuse consent required for consent to a search to be valid? NO.

SUPREME COURT DECISION: Voluntariness of consent to search is to be determined from the totality of the circumstances, of which, consent is one element. Knowledge of the right to refuse consent is not a prerequisite for voluntary consent.

REASON: "Our decision today is a narrow one. We hold only that when the subject of a search is not in custody and the State attempts to justify a search on the basis of his consent, the Fourth and Fourteenth Amendments require that it demonstrate that the consent was in fact voluntarily given and not the result of duress or coercion, expressed or implied. Voluntariness is a question of fact to be determined from all the circumstances, and while the subject's knowledge of a right to refuse is a factor to be taken into account, the prosecution is not required to demonstrate such knowledge as a prerequisite to establishing voluntary consent."

CASE SIGNIFICANCE: In *Miranda v. Arizona*, 384 U.S. 436 (1966), the Court said that the suspect must be made aware of the right to remain silent during questioning if responses to questions are later to be admissible in court. *Schneckloth* says that there is no such requirement in consent search cases. The suspect does not have to be advised that he or she has the right to refuse consent for the search to be valid. All that is required is that the consent be voluntary. The Court also said that "voluntariness is a question of fact to be determined from all the circumstances, and while the subject's knowledge of a right to refuse is a factor to be taken into account, the prosecution is not required to demonstrate such knowledge as a prerequisite to establishing voluntary consent." The police must prove that consent is voluntary; however, unlike *Miranda*, where the police must say "you have the right to remain silent," the police in consent searches do not have to say "you have the right to refuse consent."

RELATED CASES:
COOLIDGE v. NEW HAMPSHIRE, 403 U.S. 443 (1971)
DAVIS v. UNITED STATES, 328 U.S. 582 (1946)
KATZ v. UNITED STATES, 389 U.S. 347 (1967)
ZAP v. UNITED STATES, 328 U.S. 624 (1946)

UNITED STATES v. WATSON
423 U.S. 411 (1976)

FACTS: A reliable informant telephoned the postal inspector and informed him that he was in possession of a stolen credit card provided by Watson and that Watson had agreed to furnish the informant with additional cards. The informant agreed to meet with Watson and give a signal if he had additional stolen cards. When the signal was given, officers arrested Watson and took him from the restaurant where he was sitting to the street where he was given his Miranda warnings. When a search revealed no stolen credit cards on Watson, the postal inspector asked if he could look inside Watson's car. The inspector told Watson that "if I find anything, it is going to go against you." Watson agreed to the search. Using keys furnished by Watson, the car was searched and an envelope containing stolen credit cards was found. Watson was charged with and convicted of possession of stolen credit cards.

ISSUE: Can officers arrest an individual in a public place with probable cause but without an arrest warrant even if there was time to obtain a warrant? YES.

SUPREME COURT DECISION: An officer may arrest an individual in a public place without a warrant, even if there is time and opportunity to obtain one, if there is probable cause that a criminal act has been committed.

REASON: "The usual rule is that a police officer may arrest without a warrant one believed by the officer upon reasonable cause to have been guilty of a felony.....Just last term, while recognizing that maximum protection of individual rights could be assured by requiring a magistrate's review of the factual justification prior to any arrest, we stated that 'such a requirement would constitute an intolerable handicap for legitimate law enforcement' and noted that the Court 'has never invalidated an arrest supported by probable cause solely because the officers failed to secure a warrant.'" [Citations omitted.]

"The cases construing the Fourth Amendment thus reflect the ancient common-law rule that a peace officer was permitted to arrest without a warrant for a misdemeanor or felony committed in his presence as well as for a felony not committed in his presence if there was reasonable grounds for making the arrest...."

CASE SIGNIFICANCE: This case states that police officers can make an arrest in a public place without a warrant based on probable cause, hence dispensing with the warrant requirement even if the police have time to obtain a warrant. The general rule is that a warrant must be obtained before making an arrest, unless the arrest falls under one of the many exceptions to the warrant requirement. This is one of those exceptions -- arrest in a public place based on probable cause. The suspect in this case argued that the police ought to have obtained a warrant because they had time to do so. The Court ruled that the common law and the laws of most states do not require a warrant to be obtained under these circumstances.

Watson is a federal case involving postal service officers. These officers acted in accordance with a federal law that authorizes officers to "make arrest without warrant for felonies cognizable under the laws of the United States if they have reasonable grounds to believe that the person to be arrested has committed or is committing such a felony." Watson sought to have this law declared unconstitutional, in effect saying that an arrest warrant was constitutionally required whenever there was time to obtain it, even if the arrest is made in a public place. The Court disagreed, saying that such has never been required under common law, the laws of many states, or previous Court decisions. Note that this case simply says that an arrest warrant is not constitutionally required for arrests made in a public place which are based on probable cause. If a state statute requires that a warrant be obtained, then the statute must be followed. The Court noted, however, that state statutes usually do not require an arrest warrant. The rule stands, therefore, that unless a state statute or the case law provides otherwise, the police can make a warrantless arrest in a public place, based on probable cause, even if they have time to obtain a warrant.

RELATED CASES:
CARROLL v. UNITED STATES, 267 U.S. 132 (1925)
GERSTEIN v. PUGH, 420 U.S. 103 (1975)
PAYTON v. NEW YORK, 445 U.S. 573 (1980)
UNITED STATES v. SANTANA, 427 U.S. 38 (1976)

FLORIDA v. ROYER
460 U.S. 491 (1983)

FACTS: Police observed an individual in Miami International Airport who fit a so-called "drug courier profile" of being young, nervous, casually dressed, with heavy American Tourister luggage, and paying for a one-way ticket in cash under an assumed name. Based on this information, the officers approached the suspect. Upon request, but without oral consent, the suspect produced his airline ticket and driver's license with his correct name. When questioned about the discrepancy in names, the suspect responded that a friend had bought the ticket under that friend's name. Without returning the suspect's airline ticket or license, the officers then informed the suspect that he was suspected of trafficking in narcotics and requested that he follow them to a room 40 feet away. Without consent, the suspect's luggage was brought to the room. Although he did not respond to the officer's request to consent to a search of the luggage, the suspect produced a key and opened one of the suitcases. Marijuana was found in the suitcase. When the suspect said that he did not know the combination to the other suitcase but that he did not object to its being opened, the officers pried open the suitcase and found more marijuana. Royer was then informed he was under arrest. He pleaded *nolo contendere* and was convicted of felony possession of marijuana.

ISSUE: Is evidence obtained through a consent search admissible in court if the initial detention of the suspect was without probable cause, and in violation of the Fourth Amendment? NO.

SUPREME COURT DECISION: At the time the suspect consented to the search of his luggage, the detention to which he had been subjected was a more serious intrusion of his personal liberty than was allowable on mere suspicion of criminal activity; thus, the consent was tainted by illegality and could not justify the search.

REASON: "When the detectives identified themselves as narcotics agents, told respondent he was suspected of transporting narcotics, and asked him to accompany them to the police room, while retaining his airline ticket and driver's license and without indicating in any way that he was free to depart, respondent was effectively seized for purposes of the Fourth Amendment. At the time respondent produced the key to his suitcase, the detention to which he was then subjected was a more serious intrusion on his personal liberty than is allowable on mere suspicion of criminal activity. What had be-gun as a consensual inquiry in a public place escalated into an investigatory procedure in a police interrogation room, and respondent, as a practical matter, was under arrest at that time. Moreover, the detectives' conduct was more intrusive than necessary to effectuate an investigative detention other-wise authorized by the *Terry v. Ohio* line of cases."

CASE SIGNIFICANCE: Consent given after an illegal act by the police is not valid because such consent is tainted. For the consent to be valid, the police must be careful that no illegal act precedes it because once the illegal act is committed, consent cannot cure it. The only possible exception is if the taint has somehow been purged by an independant source, inevitable discov-ery, etc. In this case, however, consent did not purge the taint.

RELATED CASES:
BROWN v. ILLINOIS, 422 U.S. 590 (1975)
DUNAWAY v. NEW YORK, 442 U.S. 200 (1979)
SCHNECKLOTH v. BUSTAMONTE, 412 U.S. 218 (1973)
UNITED STATES v. MENDENHALL, 446 U.S. 544 (1980)

STONER v. CALIFORNIA
376 U.S. 483 (1964)

FACTS: Two men were described to the police by eyewitnesses after a rob-bery of a food market in California. Soon thereafter, a checkbook belonging to Stoner was found in an adjacent parking lot and turned over to the police. Checkbook stubs indicated that checks had been made out to a hotel in a nearby city. Upon checking the records in that city, the police learned that Stoner had a criminal record. The police then obtained a photograph of Stoner. Eyewitnesses identified the man in the photograph as one of the men involved in the robbery. Without an arrest or search warrant, the police went to the hotel where the suspect resided. The hotel clerk notified the police that the suspect was not in his room but consented to open the room for them. After gaining entrance to the room, the police made an extensive search and discovered articles like those described by the eyewitnesses to the robbery. Stoner was arrested two days later in another state and extradited to California. He was charged with and convicted of armed robbery.

ISSUE: May a hotel clerk give a valid consent to a warrantless search of the room of one of the occupants? NO.

SUPREME COURT DECISION: A hotel guest is entitled to protection against unreasonable searches and seizures. This cannot be waived by the consent of a hotel clerk.

REASON: "It is important to bear in mind that it was the petitioner's constitutional right which was at stake here, and not the night clerk's nor the hotel's. It was a right, therefore, which only the petitioner could waive by word or deed..."

CASE SIGNIFICANCE: A hotel guest has a reasonable expectation of privacy that cannot be waived by the hotel management simply because the management has the key. A wife can give consent to the search of a house, parents to the search of a child's room (with some exceptions), or a dormitory-mate to the search of a dormitory room; but a hotel clerk cannot give consent to search the room of a guest. Note, however, that if the police want to *arrest* a suspect in a room, the fact that access to the room was made by borrowing a key from the hotel clerk does not invalidate the arrest. The rule on consent, therefore, differs in arrest and in search cases.

RELATED CASES:
CHAPMAN v. UNITED STATES, 365 U.S. 610 (1961)
McDONALD v. UNITED STATES, 335 U.S. 451 (1948)
UNITED STATES v. JEFFERS, 342 U.S. 48 (1951)
UNITED STATES v. MATLOCK, 415 U.S. 164 (1974)

VEHICLE SEARCHES 9

CARROLL v. UNITED STATES
267 U.S. 132 (1925)

FACTS: Officers observed the automobile of Carroll while on a regular patrol from Detroit to Grand Rapids. The same officers had been in contact with Carroll twice in the four months prior to this sighting. In September, the officers attempted to buy illegal liquor from Carroll but he was alerted to their true identity and did not produce the contraband. In October, the officers recognized Carroll's automobile returning to Grand Rapids from Detroit (a city possessing an international boundary and which was known as a city from which illegal liquor was regularly imported). The officers gave chase but failed to apprehend Carroll. Carroll was later apprehended. He and his companion were ordered out of the car. No liquor was visible in the front seat of the automobile. Officers then opened the rumble seat and looked under the cushions, again finding no liquor. One of the officers then struck the "lazyback" of the seat, tore open the seat cushion, and discovered 68 bottles of gin and whiskey. Carroll was arrested and convicted of transporting intoxicating liquor.

ISSUE: May officers search an automobile without a search warrant but with probable cause that it contains illegal contraband? YES.

SUPREME COURT DECISION: The risk of the vehicle being moved from the jurisdiction, or the evidence being destroyed or carried off, justifies a warrantless search as long as such search is conducted with probable cause that the vehicle which is subject to seizure contains contraband.

REASON: "...[T]he guarantee of freedom from unreasonable searches and seizures by the Fourth Amendment has been construed, practically since the beginning of government, as recognizing a necessary difference between a search of a store, dwelling house, or other structure in respect of which a proper official warrant readily may be obtained and a search of a ship, motor boat, wagon, or automobile for contraband goods, where it is not practicable to secure a warrant, because the vehicle can be quickly moved out of the locality or jurisdiction in which the warrant must be sought."

CASE SIGNIFICANCE: The general rule is that searches may be conducted only if a warrant has been issued. There are several exceptions to this rule, however, searches of automobiles being one of them. This case, decided in 1925, created the so-called "automobile exception" to the warrant requirement by ruling that warrantless searches of motor vehicles are valid as long as there is probable cause to believe that there are seizable items in the vehicle. The justification for this exception is the mobile nature of the automobile.

RELATED CASES:
COLORADO v. BERTINE, 479 U.S. 367 (1987)
NEW YORK v. BELTON, 453 U.S. 454 (1981)
TEXAS v. BROWN, 460 U.S. 730 (1983)
UNITED STATES v. ROSS, 456 U.S. 798 (1982)

DELAWARE v. PROUSE
440 U.S. 648 (1979)

FACTS: Without observing traffic or equipment violations or suspicious activity, a police officer stopped Prouse's vehicle to check the driver's license and registration. Upon approaching the vehicle, the officer smelled marijuana. He seized a quantity of marijuana in plain view on the floor of the automobile. The officer was not acting pursuant to any departmental regulations governing spot checks. Prouse was charged with and convicted of illegal possession of a controlled substance.

ISSUE: May a police officer make a random stop of an automobile simply to check the driving license of the operator and registration of the automobile in the absence of probable cause that its occupants are engaging in illegal activity? NO.

SUPREME COURT DECISION: Stopping an automobile and detaining the driver in order to check the license and registration is unreasonable under the Fourth Amendment unless there is probable cause to believed that the motorist is unlicensed or that the automobile is in violation of equipment laws, or that its occupants are exhibiting suspicious behavior.

REASON: "The Fourth and Fourteenth Amendments are implicated in this case because stopping an automobile and detaining its occupants constitute a 'seizure' within the meaning of those Amendments, even though the purpose of the stop is limited and the resulting detention quite brief. The essential purpose of the proscriptions in the Fourth Amendment is to impose a standard of reasonableness upon the exercise of discretion by government officials, including law enforcement agents, in order to 'safeguard the privacy and security of individuals against invasions.'" [Citations omitted.]

CASE SIGNIFICANCE: This case holds that officers cannot arbitrarily stop motor vehicles without probable cause to believe that an illegality or violation has occurred or is occurring. Vehicles may be searched without warrant, but probable cause must be present. Does this mean that vehicle spot checks are illegal? Not necessarily. The Court in this case said that this decision does not preclude a state from "developing methods for spot checks that involve less intrusion or that do not involve the unconstrained exercise of discretion." For example, questioning all oncoming traffic at roadblock-type stops is valid and may be use by the police.

RELATED CASES:
TERRY v. OHIO, 392 U.S. 1 (1968)
UNITED STATES v. BRIGNONI-PONCE, 422 U.S. 873 (1975)
UNITED STATES v. MARTINEZ-FUERTE, 428 U.S. 543 (1976)
UNITED STATES v. ORTIZ, 422 U.S. 891 (1975)

NEW YORK v. BELTON
453 U.S. 454 (1981)

FACTS: Police stopped an automobile of which Belton was an occupant. A check of driver's licenses and automobile registration revealed that none of the occupants owned the vehicle or were related to the owner. The officer smelled burnt marijuana and saw an envelope marked "Supergold" on the floor of the automobile which the officer associated with marijuana. After administering the *Miranda* warnings, the officer placed the occupants under arrest, picked up the envelope, and found marijuana. He then searched the passenger compartment of the automobile and, on the back seat, found a jacket belonging to Belton. He unzipped one of the pockets of the jacket and discovered cocaine. Belton was arrested for and convicted of possession of a controlled substance.

ISSUE: Is the warrantless seizure of evidence in the passenger compartment of a car, after a lawful arrest, valid? YES.

SUPREME COURT DECISION: The police may conduct a warrantless search of the passenger compartment of a car incident to a lawful arrest. The search may include containers found within the passenger compartment. The term "container" denotes any object capable of holding another object. It includes closed or open glove compartments, consoles, or other receptacles located anywhere within the passenger compartment, as well as luggage, boxes, bags, clothing, and similar items.

REASON: "[I]n *United States v. Robinson*, 414 U.S. 218, the Court hewed a straightforward rule...in the case of a lawful custodial arrest a full search of the person is not only an exception to the warrant requirement of the Fourth Amendment, but is also a 'reasonable' search under that Amendment.... Accordingly, we hold that when a policeman has made a lawful custodial arrest of the occupant of an automobile, he may, as a contemporaneous incident of that arrest, search the passenger compartment of that automobile.... It follows from this conclusion that the police may also examine the contents of any containers found within the passenger compartment, for if the passenger compartment is within the reach of the arrestee, so also will containers in it be within his reach."

CASE SIGNIFICANCE: This case defined the extent of allowable search inside the automobile after a lawful arrest. Prior to this, there was confusion about whether the police may search parts of the automobile outside the driver's "wingspan." The Court expanded the area of allowable search to the whole passenger compartment, including the back seat; it also authorized the opening of containers found in the passenger compartment that might contain the object sought. In this case, Belton's jacket could contain prohibited drugs; its search was therefore valid. This case also authorizes the police to search the interior of the car even if the passenger has been removed from the car or no longer constitutes a danger to the police (such as when the passenger has been handcuffed). (Note, however, that the *Belton* case did not decide whether or not the trunk could also be searched. This case was decided later in *United States v. Ross*, 456 U.S. 798 [1982]).

RELATED CASES:
CARROLL v. UNITED STATES, 267 U.S. 132 (1925)
CHIMEL v. CALIFORNIA, 395 U.S. 752 (1969)
TEXAS v. BROWN, 460 U.S. 730 (1983)
UNITED STATES v. ROSS, 456 U.S. 798 (1982)

UNITED STATES v. ROSS
456 U.S. 798 (1982)

FACTS: Police received a telephone tip from a reliable informant that Ross was selling narcotics kept in the trunk of his car. The informant provided a detailed description of Ross, his automobile and the location of the sale. The police drove to the location, spotted the person and car that matched the description given by the informant and made a warrantless arrest. One of the officers found a bullet on the front seat of the automobile. Without a warrant, officers conducted a more thorough search of the interior of the automobile and discovered a pistol in the glove compartment. Ross was arrested. Officers then took Ross's keys and opened the trunk of his automobile, where they found a closed brown paper bag containing glassine bags of a substance that turned out to be heroin. The officers then drove the car to police headquarters where another warrantless search of the trunk revealed a zippered leather pouch containing cash. Ross was charged with and convicted of possession of heroin with intent to distribute.

ISSUE: After a valid arrest, may the police open the trunk of a car and containers found therein without a warrant and in the absence of exigent circumstances? YES.

SUPREME COURT DECISION: When the police have probable cause to justify a warrantless search of a car, they may search the entire car, and open the trunk and any packages or luggage found therein that could reasonably contain the items for which they have probable cause to search.

REASON: "If probable cause justifies the search of a lawfully stopped vehicle, it justifies the search of every part of the vehicle and its contents that may conceal the object of the search....The scope of a warrantless search of an automobile thus is not defined by the nature of the container in which the contraband is secreted. Rather, it is defined by the object of the search and the places in which there is probable cause to believe that it may be found."

CASE SIGNIFICANCE: The *Ross* case is important because that it further defines the scope of police authority in vehicle searches. The *Belton* case specifically refused to address the issue of whether or not the police could open the trunk of a car in connection with a search incident to a valid arrest. *Ross* addressed that issue and authorized such action. *Ross* further stated that any packages or luggage found in the car that could reasonably contain the items for which they have probable cause to search could also be opened without a warrant. *Ross* has therefore greatly expanded the scope of allowable warrantless searches, limited only by what is reasonable. Note, however, that this authorization has limits. The police may not open large items taken from the car (such as a footlocker) without a warrant if there is time to obtain one. This is because those items have identities of their own, separate and apart from the car. Also, although the police may constitutionally open smaller items without a warrant, that action may be prohibited by state law or departmental policy, which prevails over a constitutional license.

RELATED CASES:
CARROLL v. UNITED STATES, 267 U.S. 132 (1925)
HUSTY v. UNITED STATES, 282 U.S. 694 (1931)
SCHER v. UNITED STATES, 305 U.S. 251 (1938)
CHAMBERS v. MARONEY, 399 U.S. 42 (1970)

MICHIGAN v. LONG
463 U.S. 1032 (1983)

FACTS: Officers observed an automobile traveling erratically and at a high rate of speed. When the automobile swerved into a ditch, the officers stopped to investigate. They were met at the rear of the car by Long, who "appeared to be under the influence of something" and did not respond to a request to produce his license. Upon a second request Long did produce his license. After a second request to see his registration, Long began walking toward the open door of the vehicle. The officers followed him and noticed a large hunting knife on the floorboard of the vehicle. They then stopped Long and frisked him. No weapons were found. One of the officers shined his flashlight into the car and discovered marijuana. Long was then arrested. The officers then opened the unlocked trunk and discovered approximately 75 pounds of marijuana. Long was charged with and convicted of possession of marijuana.

ISSUE: May officers conduct a protective search (similar to a pat-down search authorized in *Terry v. Ohio*, 392 U.S. 1 [1968]) of the passenger compartment of a lawfully stopped vehicle to look for possible weapons? YES.

SUPREME COURT DECISION: The search of an automobile, after a valid stop and limited to those areas in which a weapon may be placed or hidden, is permissible if the officer has a reasonable belief that the suspect is dangerous and might gain immediate control of a weapon.

REASON: "[A]rticles inside the relatively narrow compass of the passenger compartment of an automobile are in fact generally, even if not inevitably, within the area into which an arrestee might reach in order to grab a weapon." (footnote and quotes omitted)...."If there is reasonable belief that the suspect is dangerous and might gain control of weapons, the officer is justified by self-protection to make search of the interior of the automobile....If, while conducting a legitimate *Terry* search of the interior of the automobile, the officer should, as here, discover contraband other than weapons, he clearly cannot be required to ignore the contraband..."

CASE SIGNIFICANCE: This case gives the police authority to conduct a limited search (similar to a pat-down search of a person) of the passenger compartment of a car if the officers have reasonable belief that they may be in danger. In this case, the officer saw a hunting knife on the floorboard of the driver's side of the car, hence justifying the search of the passenger compartment. Such search, however, must be limited to those areas in which a weapon may be placed or hidden. If, while conducting such a search, contraband or other illegal items are discovered, they can be seized and may be admitted as evidence into court. The Court added that the fact that the suspect is under the officers' control during the investigative stop does not render unreasonable their belief that the suspect could injure them. This implies that, as long as the officers have probable cause to believe that they are in danger, the search may continue even after the suspect has been placed under control, such as when the suspect has been handcuffed.

RELATED CASES:
CHIMEL v. CALIFORNIA, 395 U.S. 752 (1969)
NEW YORK v. BELTON, 453 U.S. 454 (1981)
PENNSYLVANIA v. MIMMS, 434 U.S. 106 (1977)
TERRY v. OHIO 392 U.S. 1 (1968)

UNITED STATES v. CORTEZ
449 U.S. 411 (1981)

FACTS: Based on footprints found over a period of time, officers concluded that groups of illegal immigrants were walking over a well-defined path from the Mexican border to a highway where they would be picked up by a motor vehicle. A similar set of footprints were found in each group; therefore, officers further concluded that one person was acting as a guide to these groups. Based on the times the tracks were found, officers determined that the crossings occurred on nights during the weekend when the weather was clear. Since the tracks approached the highway then turned to the east, the officers finally concluded that the vehicle would approach from and return to the east. Based on these deductions, and the fact that a particular Sunday was the first clear night in three days, officers set up surveillance on the highway. Of the 15-20 vehicles which passed the officers during their surveillance, only 2 matched the type they were looking for. As one truck passed, the officers got a partial license plate number. When the same vehicle passed them again, heading east, they pursued and stopped it. Cortez was driving the truck and a man wearing shoes with soles matching those found in the desert was a passenger. The officers told Cortez they were conducting an immigration check. In the back of the truck were six illegal immigrants. Cortez and his companion were arrested, charged with and convicted of transporting illegal aliens.

ISSUE: May objective facts and circumstantial evidence observed and collected by the police justify an investigative stop of a vehicle? YES.

SUPREME COURT DECISION: In determining probable cause to make an investigatory stop, the totality of the circumstances (meaning the whole picture) must be taken into account. The officers must, however, have a particularized, objective basis for suspecting that the individual stopped is engaged in criminal activity.

REASON: The totality of the circumstances must yield a particularized suspicion that contains two elements which must be present before the stop can occur. First, the assessment of the situation must be based on an analysis of all of the circumstances. Second, "the whole picture must yield a particularized suspicion" which raises a suspicion that the individual being stopped is engaged in criminal activity.

CASE SIGNIFICANCE: The decision to stop and frisk must be made with justification. This means that the police cannot arbitrarily stop anyone for investigative purposes. There must be a particularized and objective basis for suspecting that the person stopped has engaged in or will engage in criminal activity. Such suspicion must be based on "the whole picture" as observed by the police. In deciding to make an investigative stop, the experience and training of the law enforcement officer may be taken into account. What may look like an innocent activity to an untrained person may look otherwise to a trained officer. Such observation gives an officer a legitimate basis for suspicion which can then justify an investigative stop.

RELATED CASES:
ALMEIDA-SANCHEZ v. UNITED STATES, 413 U.S. 266 (1973)
UNITED STATES v. BRIGNONI-PONCE, 422 U.S. 873 (1975)
UNITED STATES v. MARTINEZ-FUERTE, 428 U.S. 543 (1976)
UNITED STATES v. RAMSEY, 431 U.S. 606 (1977)

CALIFORNIA v. CARNEY
471 U.S. 386 (1985)

FACTS: A police agent had uncorroborated information that Bertine's motor home was being used to exchange marijuana for sex. He then set up surveillance on the motor home. The agent observed Bertine approach a youth who accompanied him to the motor home parked in a nearby lot. Agents followed the youth after he emerged from the motor home and stopped him. The youth said that Bertine was exchanging marijuana for sex. At the request of the agents, the youth returned to the motor home and knocked on the door. When Bertine stepped out, the agents identified themselves, entered the motor home and made a search without consent or a warrant. Agents found a quantity of marijuana on a table in the motor home. Agents then arrested Bertine and impounded the motor home. A subsequent search of the motor home at the police station revealed additional marijuana. Bertine was charged with and convicted of possession of marijuana for sale.

ISSUE: May police officers make a warrantless search, based on probable cause, of a motor home located in a public place under the vehicle exception? YES.

SUPREME COURT DECISION: If a vehicle is being used on public highways or is capable of such use and it is found in a place not regularly used for residential purposes, it may be considered a vehicle under the warrantless search doctrine; thus, a warrantless search based on probable cause is justified.

REASON: "When a vehicle is being used on the highways or is capable of such use and is found stationary in a place not regularly used for residential purposes, the two justifications for the vehicle exception come into play. First, the vehicle is readily mobile, and, second, there is a reduced expectation of privacy stemming from the pervasive regulation of vehicles capable of traveling on highways. Here, while respondent's vehicle possessed some attributes of a home, it clearly falls within the vehicle exception. To distinguish between respondent's motor home and an ordinary sedan for purposes of the vehicle exception would require that the exception be applied depending on the size of the vehicle and the quality of its appointments. Moreover, to fail to apply the exception to a vehicle such as a motor home would ignore the fact that a motor home lends itself easily to use as an instrument of illicit drug traffic or other illegal activity."

CASE SIGNIFICANCE: The Court in this case held that motor homes are automobiles for the purposes of the Fourth Amendment and therefore fall under the automobile exception, meaning that they can be searched without a warrant. It is important to note, however, that this decision is limited to a motor home that is capable of being used on the road and is located in a place that is not regularly used for residential purposes. The decision specifically states that this case does not resolve whether the automobile exception would apply to a motor home "situated in a way or place that objectively indicates that it is being used as a residence." The police are better advised to treat those places as residences that generally need a search warrant.

RELATED CASES:
CADY v. DOMBROWSKI, 413 U.S. 433 (1973)
CARROLL v. UNITED STATES, 267 U.S. 132 (1925)
CARDWELL v. LEWIS, 417 U.S. 583 (1974)
UNITED STATES v. ROSS, 456 U.S. 798 (1982)

COLORADO v. BERTINE
479 U.S. 367 (1987)

FACTS: Bertine was arrested for driving under the influence of alcohol. After he was taken into custody and prior to the arrival of a tow truck to impound the van, another officer inventoried the van in accordance with departmental procedures. During the inventory search the officer opened a backpack in which he found various containers containing controlled substances, drug paraphernalia, and money. Bertine was charged with and convicted of driving under the influence of alcohol, unlawful possession of cocaine with intent to distribute, and unlawful possession of methaqualone.

ISSUE: Is evidence seized by opening a closed container without a warrant during an inventory search incident to a lawful arrest admissible in court? YES.

SUPREME COURT DECISION: Inventory searches without a warrant of the person and possession of arrested individuals are permissible under the Fourth Amendment:
    (1)   to protect an owner's property while it is under police control;
    (2)   to insure against claims of lost, stolen, or vandalized property; and,
    (3)   to protect the police from danger. Evidence found in the course of that inventory search, even if found by opening a closed backpack, is admissible in court.

REASON: "The policies behind the warrant requirement, and the related concept of probable cause, are not implicated in an inventory search, which serves the strong governmental interests in protecting an owner's property while it is in police custody, insuring against claims of lost, stolen, or vandalized property, and guarding the police from danger. There was no showing here that the police, who were following standardized caretaking procedures, acted in bad faith or for the sole purpose of investigation. Police, before inventorying a container, are not required to weigh the strength of the individual's privacy interest in the container against the possibility that the container might serve as a repository for dangerous or valuable items."

CASE SIGNIFICANCE: This case allows inventory searches without a warrant even in situations where containers must be opened. This is significant because prior to this decision it was not clear whether or not the police, in the course of an inventory search, could open a closed container. The current rule is to allow this type of inventory, as long as the police follow standardized caretaking procedures and they do not act in bad faith or for the sole purposes of an investigation. It is questionable whether or not the opening of a closed container in the absence of departmental rules authorizing the police to do so is valid. This case synthesized *South Dakota v. Opperman*, 428 U.S. 364 (1976) (inventory search of an impounded vehicle) and *Illinois v. Lafayette*, 462 U.S. 640 (1983) (inventory search of individual possessions while person is in custody).

RELATED CASES:
COOPER v. CALIFORNIA, 386 U.S. 58 (1967)
ILLINOIS v. LAFAYETTE, 462 U.S. 640 (1983)
SOUTH DAKOTA v. OPPERMAN, 428 U.S. 364 (1976)
UNITED STATES v. CHADWICK, 433 U.S. 1 (1977)

ELECTRONIC SURVEILLANCE   10

OLMSTEAD v. UNITED STATES, 277 U.S. 438 (1928)
ON LEE v. UNITED STATES, 343 U.S. 747 (1952)
BERGER v. NEW YORK, 388 U.S. 41 (1967)
KATZ v. UNITED STATES, 389 U.S. 347 (1967)
UNITED STATES v. KARO, 468 U.S. 705 (1984)

OLMSTEAD v. UNITED STATES
277 U.S. 438 (1928)

FACTS: Olmstead and co-conspirators of a huge conglomerate involved in importing and distributing illegal liquor were convicted of conspiracy to violate the National Prohibition Act. Information leading to the arrests was gathered primarily by intercepting messages from the telephones of the conspirators. The information was obtained by placing wiretaps on the phone lines outside the conspirators office and homes. The wiretaps were installed without trespass on any property of the conspirators.

ISSUE: Do telephone wiretaps violate the Fourth Amendment protection from illegal searches and seizures? NO.

SUPREME COURT DECISION: Wiretapping does not violate the Fourth Amendment unless there is some trespass into a "constitutionally protected area." (Note: This doctrine was expressly overruled by the Supreme Court in *Katz v. United States,* 389 U.S. 347 (1967).

REASON: "The [Fourth] Amendment does not forbid what was done here. There was no searching. There was no seizure. The evidence was secured by the use of the sense of hearing and that only. There was no entry of the houses or offices of the defendants...."

CASE SIGNIFICANCE: The *Olmstead* case is significant because it represents the old rule on wiretaps. This was the first major case decided by the Court on electronic surveillance and reflects the old concept that evidence obtained through a bugging device placed against a wall to overhear conversation in an adjoining office was admissible because there was no actual trespass. The rule lasted from 1928 to 1967. In 1967, the Court decided *Katz v. United States,* 389 U.S. 347, which held that any form of electronic surveillance (including wiretapping) that violates a reasonable expectation of privacy constitutes a search. Under the new rule, the search may be unreasonable even though no physical trespass occurred.

RELATED CASES:
KATZ v UNITED STATES, 389 U.S. 347 (1967)
NARDONE v. UNITED STATES, 302 U.S. 379 (1937)
SCHWARTZ v. TEXAS, 344 U.S. 199 (1952)
UNITED STATES v. NEW YORK TELEPHONE CO., 434 U.S. 159 (1977)

ON LEE v. UNITED STATES
343 U.S. 747 (1952)

FACTS: A federal "undercover agent" who was an old acquaintance and former employee of On Lee entered his laundry wearing a radio transmitter and engaged On Lee in a conversation. Self-incriminating statements made by On Lee at that time and later in another conversation were listened to on a radio receiver outside the laundry by another federal agent. Those conversations were submitted as evidence at petitioner's trial over his objection. He was convicted of conspiring to sell and selling opium.

ISSUE: Is electronic eavesdropping a violation of the Fourth Amendment's protection from unreasonable search and seizure? NO.

SUPREME COURT DECISION: There is no violation of a suspect's Fourth Amendment right if a "friend" allows the police to listen in on a conversation; hence, the evidence obtained is admissible in court.

REASON: The conduct of the officers in this case did not constitute the kind of search and seizure that is prohibited by the Fourth Amendment. There was no trespass when the undercover agent entered the suspect's place of business, and his subsequent conduct did not render his entry a trespass *ab initio* (from the beginning). The suspect here claimed that the undercover man's entrance constituted a trespass because consent was obtained by fraud, and that the other agent was a trespasser because, by means of the radio receiver outside the laundry, the agent overheard what went on inside. The Court, however, rejected these allegations.

CASE SIGNIFICANCE: This case allows the police to obtain evidence against a suspect by bugging or listening to a conversation as long as the police have the permission of one of the parties to the conversation and such practice is not prohibited by state law. The Court in this case said that the Fourth Amendment does not protect persons against supposed friends who turn out to be police informers. Thus, a person assumes the risk that whatever is said to another person may be reported by that person to the police; there being no police "search" in such cases. It follows that if the supposed "friend" allows the police to listen in on a telephone conversation with a suspect, there is no violation of the suspect's constitutional right. The evidence can be used in court.

RELATED CASES:
KATZ v. UNITED STATES, 389 U.S. 347 (1967)
LOPEZ v. UNITED STATES, 373 U.S. 427 (1963)
SILVERMAN v. UNITED STATES, 365 U.S. 505 (1961)
UNITED STATES v. WHITE, 401 U.S. 745 (1971)

BERGER v. NEW YORK
388 U.S. 41 (1967)

FACTS: Berger was indicted and convicted of conspiracy to bribe the chairman of the New York State Liquor Authority. The conviction was based on evidence obtained by eavesdropping. The orders authorizing the placement of the bugs were pursuant to a New York State statute on electronic eavesdropping. This statute allowed the Attorney General, a District Attorney, or any police officer above the rank of Sergeant to issue the order. The order must describe who is to be bugged and the general information sought, but it does not require the particular conversation or information be described. Finally, the order may be issued for up to a two-month period with no provisions for halting the search once the specific information is found, and it has no provisions for the return of information gathered.

ISSUE: Did the New York state statute authorizing electronic eavesdropping violate the Fourth Amendment guarantee against unreasonable searches and seizures? YES.

SUPREME COURT DECISION: Electronic devices used to capture a conversation constitute a search under the Fourth Amendment. The New York State statute authorizing eavesdropping without describing the particular conversation sought was too broad and did not contain sufficient safeguards against unwarranted invasions of constitutional rights.

REASON: "The Fourth Amendment commands that a warrant issue not only upon probable cause supported by oath or affirmation, but also 'particularly describing the place to be searched, and the person or things to be seized.' New York's statute lacks particularization. It merely says that a warrant may issue on reasonable ground to believe that evidence of crime may be obtained. It lays down no requirement for particularity in the warrant as to what specific crime has been or is being committed, nor 'the place to be searched,' or 'the person or things to be seized' as specifically required by the Fourth Amendment. The need for particularity and evidence of reliability in the showing required when judicial authorization of a search is sought is especially great in the case of eavesdropping. By its very nature eavesdropping involves an intrusion on privacy that is broad in scope. As was said in *Osborn v. United States*, 385 U.S. 323 (1966), the indiscriminate use of such devices in law enforcement raises grave constitutional questions under the Fourth and Fifth Amendments, and imposes a heavier responsibility on the Court in its supervision of the fairness procedures..."

CASE SIGNIFICANCE: The *Berger* case was decided in 1967, one year prior to the enactment of Title III of the Omnibus Crime Control and Safe Streets Act. The Court in this case spelled out the six requirements for a state law authorizing electronic surveillance to be constitutionally valid. These are:

1. The warrant must describe with particularity the conversations that are to be overheard;
2. There must be a showing of probable cause to believe that a specific crime has been or is being committed;
3. The wiretap must be for a limited period, although extensions may be obtained by adequate showing;
4. The suspects whose conversations are to be overheard must be named in the judicial order;
5. A return must be made to the court, showing what conversations were intercepted; and
6. The wiretapping must terminate when the desired information has been obtained.

These six requirements have since, in effect, been enacted into law by Title III, along with many other provisions. The *Berger* case is important in that:

(1) it tells us that overly broad eavesdropping statutes are unconstitutional; and,
(2) it laid out what state statutes need in order to be valid.

The *Berger* case has since lost some of its value as precedent because of the passage of Title III.

RELATED CASES:
LOPEZ v. UNITED STATES, 373 U.S. 427 (1963)
OSBORN v. UNITED STATES, 385 U.S. 323 (1966)
SGRO v. UNITED STATES, 287 U.S. 206 (1932)
SILVERMAN v. UNITED STATES, 365 U.S. 505 (1961)

KATZ v. UNITED STATES
389 U.S. 347 (1967)

FACTS: Katz was convicted of transmitting wagering information across state lines. The evidence against Katz consisted of a conversation overheard by FBI agents who had attached an electronic listening device to the outside of a public telephone booth from which the calls were made.

ISSUE: Is a public telephone booth a constitutionally protected area such that evidence collected by an electronic listening or recording device is obtained in violation of the right to privacy of the user of the booth?   YES.

SUPREME COURT DECISION: Any form of electronic surveillance, including wiretapping, that violates a reasonable expectation of privacy, constitutes a search. No physical trespass is required.

REASON: "The government stresses the fact that the telephone booth from which the petitioner made his call was constructed partly of glass, so that he was as visible after he entered it as he would have been if he had remained outside. But what he sought to exclude when he entered the booth was not the intruding eye, it was the uninvited ear. He did not shed his right to do so simply because he made his calls from a place where he might be seen. No less than an individual in a business office, in a friends's apartment, or in a taxicab, a person in a telephone booth may rely upon the protection of the Fourth Amendment. One who occupies it, shuts the door behind him, and pays the toll that permits him to place a call is surely entitled to assume that the words he utters into the mouthpiece will not be broadcast to the world. To read the Constitution more narrowly is to ignore the vital role that the public telephone has come to play in private communication."

CASE SIGNIFICANCE: The Katz decision expressly overruled the decision 39 years earlier in *Olmstead v. United States*, 277 U.S. 348 (1928), which held that wiretapping did not violate the Fourth Amendment unless there was some trespass into a "constitutionally protected area." In *Katz* the Court said that the coverage of the Fourth Amendment does not depend on the presence or absence of a physical intrusion into a given enclosure. The current test is that a search exists, and therefore comes under the Fourth Amendment protection, whenever there is a "reasonable expectation of privacy."

The concept that the Constitution "protects people rather than places" is very significant because it makes the protection of the Fourth Amendment "portable," meaning that it is carried by persons wherever they go as long as their behavior and circumstances are such that they are entitled to a reasonable expectation of privacy. This was made clear by the Court when it said that "No less than an individual in a business office, in a friend's apartment, or in a taxicab, a person in a telephone booth may rely upon the protection of the Fourth Amendment. One who occupies it, shuts the door behind him, and pays the toll that permits him to place a call is surely entitled to assume that the words he utters into the mouthpiece will not be broadcast to the world." *Katz* has, therefore, made a significant change in the concept of the right to privacy and has greatly expanded the coverage of that right, particularly as applied to Fourth Amendment cases. It is the current standard by which the legality of search and seizure cases are tested.

RELATED CASES:
BERGER v. UNITED STATES, 388 U.S. 41 (1967)
OSBORN v. UNITED STATES, 385 U.S. 323 (1966)
SILVERMAN v. UNITED STATES, 365 U.S. 505 (1961)
UNITED STATES v. DONOVAN, 429 U.S. 413 (1977)

———

UNITED STATES v. KARO
468 U.S. 705 (1984)

FACTS: Upon learning that Karo and co-conspirators had ordered ether from a government informant to be used in extracting cocaine from clothing imported into the United States, government agents obtained a court order authorizing the installation of a beeper in one of the cans. With the informant's consent, Drug Enforcement Administration agents substituted one of their cans containing a beeper for one of the cans to be delivered to respondent. Over several months, the beeper enabled the agents to monitor the can's movement to a variety of locations, including several private residences and two commercial storage facilities. Agents obtained a search warrant for one of the homes relying in part on information derived through the use of the beeper. Based on the evidence obtained during the search, Karo and co-conspirators were arrested and charged with various drug offenses.

ISSUE: Did the monitoring of a beeper without a warrant violate the defendant's Fourth Amendment rights? YES.

SUPREME COURT DECISION: The warrantless monitoring of a beeper in a private residence violates the Fourth Amendment rights of individuals to privacy in their own homes and therefore cannot be conducted without a warrant. (The Court, however, reversed the decision on other grounds).

REASON: "The monitoring of a beeper in a private residence, a location not opened to visual surveillance, violates the Fourth Amendment rights of those who have a justifiable interest in the privacy of the residence. Here, if a DEA agent had entered the house in question without a warrant to verify that the ether was in the house, he would have engaged in an unreasonable search within the meaning of the Fourth Amendment. The result is the same where, without a warrant, the government surreptitiously uses a beeper to obtain information that it could not have obtained from outside the curtilage of the house. There is no reason in this case to deviate from the general rule that a search of a house should be conducted pursuant to a warrant."

CASE SIGNIFICANCE: A year earlier, in *United States v. Knotts*, 459 U.S. 817 (1983), the Court held that the use by the police of beepers in a car on a public road does not constitute a search because there is no reasonable expectation of privacy. Moreover, the Court added that the Fourth Amendment does not prohibit the police from supplementing their sensory faculties with technological aids to help police identify a car's location. The *Karo* and *Knotts* cases were decided differently because their facts were different. In *Knotts*, the agents learned nothing from the beeper that they could not have visually observed, hence there was no Fourth Amendment violation. Moreover, the monitoring in *Knotts* occurred in a public place, whereas the beeper in *Karo* intruded on the privacy of a home. The two cases are, therefore, complementary, not inconsistent, in legal principles.

The Court held in dicta that a warrant for the monitoring of a beeper should contain the:
(1) the object into which the beeper would be installed,
(2) the circumstances leading to the request for the beeper, and
(3) the length of time for which beeper surveillance is requested.

RELATED CASES:
BERGER v. NEW YORK, 388 U.S. 41 (1967)
KATZ v. UNITED STATES, 389 U.S. 347 (1967)
SILVERMAN v. UNITED STATES, 365 U.S. 505 (1961)
UNITED STATES v. KNOTTS, 460 U.S. 276 (1983)

PLAIN VIEW AND
OPEN FIELDS SEARCHES 11

TEXAS v. BROWN, 460 U.S. 730 (1983)
OLIVER v. UNITED STATES, 466 U.S. 170 (1984)
CALIFORNIA v. CIRAOLO, 476 U.S. 207 (1986)
UNITED STATES v. DUNN, 480 U.S. 294 (1987)
ARIZONA v. HICKS, 480 U.S. 321 (1987)

TEXAS v. BROWN
460 U.S. 730 (1983)

FACTS: An officer stopped Brown's vehicle at night at a routine driver's license checkpoint. The officer asked Brown for his driver's license and shined his flashlight into the automobile. When Brown withdrew his hand from his pocket, the officer observed an opaque, green party balloon, which was knotted one-half inch from the tip, fall from Brown's hand onto the seat. Based on his experience the officer knew that such balloons frequently contained narcotics. Responding to the officer's request to produce a driver's license, Brown reached across and opened the glove compartment. The officer shifted his position to get a better view of the glove compartment and observed several small plastic vials, a quantity of a white powdery substance, and an open package of party balloons. After rummaging through the glove compartment, Brown informed the officer that he did not have a driver's license. The officer picked up the balloon which had a white powdery substance in the tied off portion and showed it to another officer who also recognized the balloon as one possibly containing narcotics. The officers placed Brown under arrest. A search of Brown's vehicle incident to the arrest revealed several plastic bags containing a green leafy substance and a bottle of milk sugar. Brown was charged with and convicted of possession of heroin.

ISSUE: Must an officer be able to immediately recognize an object in plain view as contraband or evidence of criminal activity before it may be seized under the "plain view doctrine?" NO.

SUPREME COURT DECISION: Items must be "immediately recognizable" as subject to seizure if they are to fall under the "plain view" doctrine, but, "certain knowledge" that incriminating evidence is involved is not necessary. Probable cause is sufficient to justify a seizure. The use of a flashlight by an officer during the evening to look into the inside of a car does not constitute a search under the Fourth Amendment. The items discovered still fall under plain view.

REASON: "In the *Coolidge* [*v. New Hampshire*, 403 U.S. 443 (1970)] plurality's view, the 'plain view' doctrine permits the warrantless seizure by police of private possessions where three requirements are satisfied. First, the police officer must lawfully make an 'initial intrusion' or otherwise properly be in a position from which he can view a particular area. Second, the officer must discover incriminating evidence 'inadvertently,' which is to say, he may not 'know in advance the location of [certain] evidence and intend to seize it,' relying on the plain-view doctrine only as a pretext. Finally, it must be 'immediately apparent' to the police that the items they observe may be evidence of a crime, contraband, or otherwise subject to seizure." [Citations omitted.] The "immediately apparent" language in *Coolidge*, however, does not require an officer to "know" that items are contraband or evidence of criminal activity, probable cause is sufficient.

CASE SIGNIFICANCE: There are four basic elements of the "plain view" doctrine. They are:
  (1) awareness of the item must be gained solely through the sense of sight;
  (2) the officer must be legally present in the place from which he or she see the items;
  (3) discovery of the items must be inadvertent; and,
  (4) the items must be immediately recognizable as subject to seizure.

This case clarifies the fourth requirement, saying that "immediate recognizability" does not mean "certain knowledge." All that is needed is probable cause. In this case, the officer shined his flashlight into the car's interior and saw the driver holding an opaque green party balloon, knotted about one-half inch from the tip. The officer also saw white powder in the open glove compartment. In court, the officer testified that he had learned from experience that inflated, tied-off balloons are often used to transport narcotics. The Court concluded that the officer had probable cause to believe that the balloon contained narcotics and that a warrantless seizure was, therefore, justified under the plain view doctrine. Significantly, the Court said that "plain view is perhaps better understood...not as an independent exception to the warrant clause, but simply as an extension of whatever the prior justification for an officer's access to an object may be."

RELATED CASES:
ARIZONA v. HICKS, 480 U.S. 321 (1987)
COOLIDGE v. NEW HAMPSHIRE, 403 U.S. 443 (1971)
HARRIS v. UNITED STATES, 390 U.S. 234 (1968)
UNITED STATES v. LEE, 274 U.S. 559 (1927)

OLIVER v. UNITED STATES
466 U.S. 170 (1984)

FACTS: Acting on reports that marijuana was grown on petitioner's farm, but without a search warrant, probable cause, or exigent circumstances, police officers went to the farm to investigate. They drove past Oliver's house to a locked gate with a "No Trespassing" sign but with a footpath around one side. Officers followed the footpath around the gate and found a field of marijuana over a mile from petitioner's house. Oliver was charged with and convicted of manufacturing a controlled substance.

ISSUE: Does the "open fields" doctrine apply when the property owner attempts to establish a reasonable expectation of privacy by posting a "No Trespassing" sign, using a locked gate, and when marijuana is located more than a mile from the house?   YES.

SUPREME COURT DECISION: Because open fields are accessible to the public and the police in ways that a home, office, or commercial structure would not be, and because fences or "No Trespassing" signs do not effectively bar the public from viewing open fields, the expectation of privacy by an owner of an open field does not exist. Consequently, the police may enter and search unoccupied or underdeveloped areas outside the curtilage without either a warrant or probable cause.

REASON: "The test of a reasonable expectation of privacy is not whether the individual attempts to conceal criminal activity, but whether the government's intrusion infringes upon the personal and societal values protected by the Fourth Amendment. Because open fields are accessible to the public and because fences or 'No Trespassing' signs, etc. are not effective bars to public view of open fields, the expectation of privacy does not exist and police are justified in searching these areas without a warrant."

CASE SIGNIFICANCE: This case makes clear that the "reasonable expectation of privacy" doctrine under the Fourth Amendment, as established in *Katz v. United States*, 389 U.S. 347 (1967), does not apply when the property involved is an open field. The Court stressed that steps taken to protect privacy, such as planting the marijuana on secluded land and erecting a locked gate (but with a footpath along one side) and posting "No Trespassing" signs around the property, do not establish any reasonable expectation of privacy.

This case allows law enforcement officers to make warrantless entries and searches without probable cause in open fields, thus affording them greater access to remote places where prohibited plants or drugs might be concealed.

RELATED CASES:
CALIFORNIA v. CIRAOLO, 476 U.S. 207 (1986)
HESTER v. UNITED STATES, 265 U.S. 57 (1924)
KATZ v. UNITED STATES, 389 U.S. 347 (1967)
RAKAS v. ILLINOIS, 439 U.S. 128 (1978)

CALIFORNIA v. CIRAOLO
476 U.S. 207 (1986)

FACTS: After receiving an anonymous telephone tip that Ciraolo was growing marijuana in his backyard, police went to his residence to investigate. Realizing that the area in question could not be viewed from ground level, officers used a private plane and flew over the home at an altitude prescribed by law. Officers trained in the detection of marijuana readily identified marijuana plants growing in Ciraolo's yard. Based on that information and an aerial photograph of the area, officers obtained a search warrant for the premises. A search was made pursuant to the warrant and numerous marijuana plants were seized. Ciraolo was charged with and convicted of cultivation of marijuana.

ISSUE: May officers make an aerial observation of an area within the curtilage of a home without a search warrant? YES.

SUPREME COURT DECISION: The Constitutional protection against unreasonable search and seizure is not violated by the naked-eye aerial observation by the police of a suspect's backyard, which is a part of the curtilage.

REASON: "That the area is within the curtilage does not itself bar all police observation. The Fourth Amendment protection of the home has never been extended to require law enforcement officers to shield their eyes when passing by a home on public thoroughfares. Nor does the mere fact that an individual has taken measures to restrict some views of his activities preclude an officer's observations from a public vantage point where he has a right to be and which renders the activities clearly visible."

CASE SIGNIFICANCE: The term "curtilage" refers to the grounds and buildings immediately surrounding a dwelling. Ordinarily, curtilage is not considered an open field and hence is protected against unreasonable searches and seizures. This means that searching a curtilage requires a warrant. In this case, however, the Court said there was no need for a warrant because the search was in the form of a naked-eye aerial observation of a suspect's backyard and is, therefore, less intrusive. The Court said that the fact that the area is with the curtilage does not in itself prohibit all police observation. This case therefore expands police power to search a curtilage without a warrant, but only if the search is aerial in nature.

RELATED CASES:
BOYD v. UNITED STATES, 116 U.S. 616 (1886)
DOW CHEMICAL CO. v. UNITED STATES, 476 U.S. 227 (1986)
FLORIDA v. RILEY, 109 S. Ct. 693 (1989)
OLIVER v. UNITED STATES, 466 U.S. 170 (1984)

UNITED STATES v. DUNN
480 U.S. 294 (1987)

FACTS: After learning that a co-defendant purchased large quantities of chemicals and equipment used in the manufacture of controlled substances, drug agents obtained a warrant to place an electronic tracking beeper in some of the equipment. The beeper ultimately led agents to Dunn's farm. The farm was encircled by a perimeter fence with several interior fences of the type used to hold livestock. Without a warrant, officers entered the premises over the perimeter fence, interior fences, and a wooden fence which encircled a barn, approximately 50 yards from respondent's home. The officers were led to the barn by the odor of chemicals and the sound of a running motor. Without entering the barn, officers stood at a locked gate and shined a flashlight into the barn where they observed what appeared to be a drug laboratory. Officers returned twice the next day to confirm the presence of the laboratory, each time without entering the barn. Based on information gained from these observations, officers obtained a search warrant and seized the drug lab from the barn and a quantity of controlled substances from the house. Dunn was charged with and convicted of conspiracy to manufacture controlled substances.

ISSUE: Is a barn located approximately 50 yards from a house and surrounded by a fence different from that of the house, part of the curtilage and, therefore, cannot be searched without a warrant? NO.

SUPREME COURT DECISION: The barn that was searched by the police was not a part of the curtilage and, therefore, the warrantless search by the police was valid. Whether or not an area is considered a part of the curtilage of a home rests on four factors:
    (1)   the proximity of the area to the home;
    (2)   whether the area is in an enclosure surrounding the home;
    (3)   the nature and uses of the area;
    (4)   and the steps taken to conceal the area from public view.

Applying these factors, the barn in this case could not be considered a part of the curtilage.

REASON: "Under *Oliver* [*v. United States*, 466 U.S. 170 (1984)] and *Hester* [*v. United States*, 265 U.S. 57 (1924)], there is no constitutional difference between police observations conducted while in a public place and while standing in an open field."

CASE SIGNIFICANCE: This case is important because, for the first time, the Court laid out the standards for determining whether or not a particular building falls within the curtilage of the main house. Applying the four factors enumerated above, the Court concluded that the barn searched by the police did not fall within the curtilage of the main building and, therefore, did not need a warrant to be searched. These four factors take into account such elements of reason as proximity, enclosure, uses, and steps taken to protect the area. The problem with these factors is that they are necessarily subjective and therefore lend themselves to imprecise application. Nonetheless, they are an improvement over the complete lack of guidelines under which the lower courts decided cases prior to this one.

RELATED CASES:
BOYD v. UNITED STATES, 116 U.S. 616 (1886)
CALIFORNIA v. CIRAOLO, 476 U.S. 207 (1986)
HESTER v. UNITED STATES, 265 U.S. 57 (1924)
OLIVER v. UNITED STATES, 466 U.S. 170 (1984)

ARIZONA v. HICKS
480 U.S. 321 (1987)

FACTS: A bullet fired through the floor of Hicks's apartment, injuring a man below, prompted the police to enter Hicks's apartment to search for the shooter, weapons, and other victims. The police discovered three weapons and a stocking cap mask. An officer noticed several pieces of stereo equipment which seemed to be out of place in the ill-appointed apartment. Based on this suspicion, he read and recorded the serial numbers of the equipment, moving some of the pieces in the process. A call to police headquarters verified that one of the pieces of equipment was stolen. A subsequent check of the serial numbers of the other pieces of equipment revealed they were also stolen. A search warrant was then obtained and the other equipment seized. Hicks was charged with and convicted of robbery.

ISSUE: May an officer make a "plain view" search with less than probable cause to believe the items being searched are contraband or evidence of criminal activity? NO.

SUPREME COURT DECISION: Probable cause to believe that items being searched are, in fact, contraband or evidence of criminal activity is required for the items to be searched under the "plain view" doctrine.

REASON: "...[M]oving the equipment...did constitute a 'search' separate and apart from the search for the shooter, victims, and weapons that was the lawful objective of [the officer's] entry into the apartment. Merely inspecting those parts of the turntable that came into view during the latter search would not have constituted an independent search, because it would have produced no additional invasion of respondent's privacy interest. But taking action, unrelated to the objectives of the authorized intrusion, which exposed to view concealed portions of the apartment or its contents, did produce a new invasion of respondent's privacy unjustified by the exigent circumstance that validated the entry."

CASE SIGNIFICANCE: The "plain view" doctrine states that items within the sight of an officer who is legally in the place from which the view is made, and who had no prior knowledge that the items were present, may properly be seized without a warrant as long as the items are immediately recognizable as subject to seizure. This case holds that even after the officer has seen an object in plain view, he or she may not search or seize it unless there is probable cause to believe that the object is contraband or stolen property, or that it is useful as evidence in court. Therefore, if, at the moment the object is picked up, the officer did not have probable cause but only "reasonable suspicion" (as was the case here), the seizure is illegal. The "plain view" doctrine as the basis for warrantless seizure may be invoked by the police only if there is probable cause to believe that the item is contraband or useful evidence; it may not be invoked based on "reasonable suspicion" or any other level of certainty that is less than probable cause.

RELATED CASES:
COOLIDGE v. NEW HAMPSHIRE, 403 U.S. 443 (1971)
ILLINOIS v. ANDREAS, 463 U.S. 765 (1983)
MARYLAND v MACON, 472 U.S. 463 (1985)
MINCEY v. ARIZONA, 437 U.S. 385 (1978)

LINEUPS AND
OTHER PRETRIAL
IDENTIFICATION PROCEDURES   12

UNITED STATES v. WADE, 388 U.S. 218 (1967)
FOSTER v. CALIFORNIA, 394 U.S. 440 (1969)
KIRBY v. ILLINOIS, 406 U.S. 682 (1972)
UNITED STATES v. DIONISIO, 410 U.S. 1 (1973)

UNITED STATES v. WADE
388 U.S. 218 (1967)

FACTS: A man with a small piece of tape on each side of his face entered a bank and pointed a pistol at a cashier and the vice-president of the bank, and forced them to fill a pillow case with the bank's money. The man then drove away with an accomplice. An indictment was returned against Wade and others involved in the robbery. Wade was arrested and counsel was appointed. Fifteen days later, without notice to his counsel, Wade was placed in a lineup to be viewed by the bank personnel. Both employees identified Wade as the robber; in court they admitted seeing Wade in the custody of officials prior to the lineup. At trial, the bank personnel re-identified Wade as the robber and the prior lineup identifications were admitted as evidence. Wade was convicted of bank robbery.

ISSUE: Should the courtroom identification of an accused be excluded as evidence because the accused was exhibited to the witness before trial at a post-indictment lineup conducted for identification purposes without notice to and in the absence of accused's appointed lawyer? YES.

SUPREME COURT DECISION: A police lineup or other "face-to-face" confrontation after the accused has been formally charged with a crime is considered a "critical stage of the proceedings;" therefore, the accused has the right to have counsel present. The absence of counsel during such proceedings renders the evidence obtained inadmissible.

REASON: "Since it appears that there is grave potential for prejudice, intentional or not, in the pretrial lineup, which may not be capable of reconstruction at trial, and since presence of counsel itself can often avert prejudice and assure a meaningful confrontation at trial, there can be little doubt that for Wade the post-indictment lineup was a critical stage of the prosecution at which he was 'as much entitled to such aid [of counsel]...as at the trial itself.' Thus both Wade and his counsel should have been notified of the impending lineup, and counsel's presence should have been requisite to conduct of the lineup, absent an 'intelligent waiver.'"

CASE SIGNIFICANCE: The *Wade* case settled the issue of whether or not an accused has a right to counsel after the filing of a formal charge. The standard used by the Court was whether or not the identification was part of the "critical stage of the proceedings." The Court, however, did not say exactly what this phrase meant; hence lower courts did not know where to draw the line. In a subsequent case, *Kirby v. Illinois* (see brief in this book), the Court said that any pretrial identification prior to the filing of a formal charge was not part of the "critical stage of the proceeding," and therefore no counsel was required. The *Wade* case also did not authoritatively state what is meant by "formal charge," so that phrase has also been subject to varying interpretations, depending on state law or practice.

RELATED CASES:
GILBERT v. CALIFORNIA, 388 U.S. 263 (1967)
MOORE v. ILLINOIS, 434 U.S. 220 (1977)
STOVAL v. DENNO, 388 U.S. 293 (1967)
UNITED STATES v. ASH, 413 U.S. 300 (1973)

FOSTER v. CALIFORNIA
394 U.S. 440 (1969)

FACTS: The day after a robbery, one of the robbers, Foster, surrendered to the police and implicated the other two involved. Foster was placed in a lineup with two other men and viewed by the only witness to the robbery, the night manager of the office. Foster was wearing a jacket similar to the one worn by the robber and was several inches taller than either of the two men. The witness could not positively identify Foster as the robber and asked to speak with him. Foster was brought into an office alone and was seated at a table with the witness; still the witness could not positively identify Foster as the robber. A week to ten days later the witness viewed a second lineup of Foster and four completely different men. This time the witness positively identified Foster as the robber. The witness testified to the identification of Foster in the lineups and repeated the identification in court. Foster was charged with and convicted of robbery.

ISSUE: Did the lineup conducted by the police violate Foster's constitutional rights? YES.

SUPREME COURT DECISION: Lineups which are so suggestive as to make the resulting identifications virtually inevitable violate a suspect's constitutional right to due process.

REASON: "This case presents a compelling example of unfair lineup procedures. In the first lineup arranged by the police, petitioner stood out from the other two men by the contrast of his height and by the fact that he was wearing a leather jacket similar to that worn by the robber. When this did not lead to positive identification, the police permitted a one-to-one confrontation between petitioner and the witness.... Even after this the witness' identification of petitioner was tentative. So some days later another lineup was arranged. Petitioner was the only person in this lineup who had also participated in the first lineup....This finally produced a definitive identification.... The suggestive elements in this identification procedure made it all but inevitable that [the witness] would identify petitioner whether or not he was in fact 'the man.' In effect, the police repeatedly said to the witness, 'This is the man.' This procedure so undermined the reliability of the eyewitness identification as to violate due process."

CASE SIGNIFICANCE: This case tells the police how *not* to conduct a lineup. Lineups are important to the accused as well as to the police and, therefore, must be conducted properly. Any lineup that practically identifies the suspect for the witness is unfair to the suspect and violates due process. The procedure followed by the police in this case practically ensured the suspect's identification by the witness in that:

(1) the suspect was much taller than the other two people in the lineup;
(2) only the suspect was wearing a leather jacket similar to that worn by the robber;
(3) there was a subsequent one-to-one confrontation between the suspect and the witness; and,
(4) in the second lineup, the suspect was the only person who had participated in the first lineup.

Lineups must be fair to the suspect; otherwise, the due process rights of the suspect are violated. A fair lineup is one which guarantees no bias against the suspect.

RELATED CASES:
MANSON v. BRATHWAITE, 432 U.S. 98 (1977)
SIMMONS v. UNITED STATES, 390 U.S. 377 (1968)
STOVAL v. DENNO, 388 U.S. 293 (1967)
UNITED STATES v. WADE, 388 U.S. 218 (1967)

KIRBY v. ILLINOIS
406 U.S. 682 (1972)

FACTS: A man reported that two men robbed him of a wallet containing traveler's checks and a social security card. The following day, two police officers stopped Kirby and a companion. When asked for identification, Kirby produced a wallet that contained three traveler's checks and the social security card bearing the name of the man. The officers took Kirby and his companion to the police station. Only after arriving at the police station and checking the records there did the arresting officers learn of the robbery. The man was then brought to the police station. Immediately upon entering the room in the police station where Kirby and his companion were seated, the man positively identified them as the men who had robbed him. No lawyer was present in the room and neither Kirby nor his companion asked for legal assistance, nor were they advised by the police of any right to the presence of counsel. Kirby was convicted of robbery.

ISSUE: Is a suspect entitled to the presence and advice of a lawyer during pretrial identification? NO.

SUPREME COURT DECISION: There is no right to counsel at police lineups or identification procedures prior to the time the suspect is formally charged with the crime.

REASON: "The initiation of judicial criminal proceedings is far from mere formalism. It is the starting point of our whole adversarial system of criminal justice. For it is only then that the government has committed itself to prosecute, and only then that the adverse positions of government and defendant have solidified. It is then that a defendant finds himself faced with the prosecutorial forces of organized society, and immersed in the intricacies of substantive and procedural criminal law. It is this point, therefore, that marks the commencement of the 'criminal prosecutions' to which alone the explicit guarantees of the Sixth Amendment are applicable."

CASE SIGNIFICANCE: *Kirby* was decided five years after *United States v. Wade*. It clarified an issue that was not directly resolved in *Wade*, whether the ruling in *Wade* applied to cases in which the lineup or pretrial identification takes place prior to the filing of a formal charge. The court answered this question in the negative, saying that what happened in *Kirby* was a matter of routine police investigation, hence not considered a "critical stage of the prosecution." The Court reasoned that a post-indictment lineup is a "critical stage" whereas a pre-indictment lineup is not.

RELATED CASES:
GILBERT v. CALIFORNIA, 388 U.S. 263 (1967)
STOVAL v. DENNO, 388 U.S. 293 (1967)
UNITED STATES v. ASH, 413 U.S. 300 (1973)
UNITED STATES v. WADE, 388 U.S. (1967)

UNITED STATES v. DIONISIO
410 U.S. 1 (1973)

FACTS: In the course of its investigation into illegal gambling, a grand jury received voice recordings obtained pursuant to court orders. The grand jury subpoenaed 20 people, including Dionisio, and compelled them to provide voice exemplars for comparison with the intercepted messages. Each witness was advised that he was a potential defendant in the investigation and was given the right to have an attorney present during the taping. Each witness was provided a copy of the transcript of the messages and was compelled to read the transcript into a recording device. Dionisio and others refused to provide the voice exemplars. The government filed petitions in the District Court to compel the witnesses to make the voice recordings, which the court did. Dionisio maintained his refusal to provide the voice exemplars and was found in civil contempt and was incarcerated until he complied with the order or for 18 months.

ISSUE: May a person be required to appear before a grand jury, and is the providing of voice exemplars compelled by a grand jury for the purpose of comparison with intercepted messages a violation of the Fourth Amendment protection from unreasonable search and seizure and the Fifth Amendment protection from self-incrimination? NO.

SUPREME COURT DECISION:
1. Any person may be required against his or her will to appear before a grand jury. Such is not a form of seizure protected by the Fourth Amendment.

2.   Suspects may be required by the police to give voice exemplars. Such requirement does not violate the Fifth Amendment protection from self-incrimination.

REASON:
1.   "It is clear that a subpoena to appear before a grand jury is not a 'seizure' in the Fourth Amendment sense, even though that summons may be inconvenient or burdensome... [W]e again acknowledge what has long been recognized, that 'citizens generally are not constitutionally immune from grand jury subpoenas.... These are recent reaffirmations of the historically grounded obligation of every person to appear and give his evidence before the grand jury. 'The personal sacrifices involved is a part of the necessary contribution of the individual to the welfare of the public.'"

2.   "The physical characteristics of a person's voice, its tone and manner, as opposed to the context of a specific conversation, are constantly exposed to the public. Like a man's facial characteristics, or handwriting, his voice is repeatedly produced for others to hear. No person can have a reasonable expectation that others will not know the sound of his voice, any more than he can reasonably expect that his face will be a mystery to the world."

CASE SIGNIFICANCE: A suspect may be required to appear before a grand jury and can be forced to give a voice exemplar for the purposes of comparison with an actual voice recording. Appearance before the grand jury is not a form of search and the giving of a voice exemplar is not a form of seizure that is protected by the Fourth Amendment. Appearance before a grand jury is a duty; therefore, non-appearance cannot be a constitutional right. In the case of a person's voice, there is no reasonable expectation of privacy to it because a voice is constantly exposed and available to the public. Although not discussed directly in this case, the Court considers voice exemplars to be a form of physical (as opposed to testimonial) self-incrimination and, therefore, not protected by the Fifth Amendment prohibition against self-incrimination. It is important for police officers to know that the prohibition against self-incrimination applies only to testimonial and not to physical self-incrimination. Physical self-incrimination would therefore compel a person to appear in a police lineup against his or her will.

RELATED CASES:
DAVIS v. MISSISSIPPI, 394 U.S. 721 (1969)
SCHMERBER v. CALIFORNIA, 384 U.S. 757 (1966)
TERRY v. OHIO, 392 U.S. 1 (1968)
WINSTON v. LEE, 470 U.S. 753 (1985)

USE OF FORCE 13

TENNESSEE v. GARNER, 471 U.S. 1 (1985)
GRAHAM v. CONNOR, 109 S. Ct. 1865 (1989)

TENNESSEE v. GARNER
471 U.S. 1 (1985)

FACTS: Memphis police officers were dispatched to answer a "prowler inside call." At the scene they saw a woman standing on her porch and gesturing toward the adjacent house. She told them she had heard glass breaking and that someone was breaking in next door. While one officer radioed the dispatcher, the other went behind the adjacent house. He heard a door slam and saw someone run across the backyard. The fleeing suspect, Edward Garner, stopped at a six-foot-high chain-link fence at the edge of the yard. With the aid of a flashlight, the officer was able to see Garner's face and hands. He saw no sign of a weapon, and, though not certain, was "reasonably sure" that Garner was unarmed. While Garner was crouched at the base of the fence, the officer called out "Police, halt" and took a few steps toward him. Garner then began to climb over the fence. Believing that if Garner made it over the fence he would elude capture, the officer shot him. Garner was taken by ambulance to a hospital where he died. Ten dollars and a purse taken from the house were found on his body.

ISSUE: Is the use of deadly force to prevent the escape of an individual suspected of a non-violent felony constitutional? NO.

SUPREME COURT DECISION: Deadly force may not be used unless it is necessary to prevent the escape and the officer has probable cause to believe that the suspect poses a significant threat of death or serious physical injury to the officer or others.

REASON: "The use of deadly force to prevent the escape of all felony suspects, whatever the circumstances, is constitutionally unreasonable. It is not better that all felony suspects die than that they escape. Where the suspect poses no immediate threat to the officer and no threat to others, the harm resulting from failing to apprehend him does not justify the use of deadly force to do so. It is no doubt unfortunate when a suspect who is in sight escapes, but the fact that the police arrive a little late or are a little slower of foot does not always justify killing the suspect. A police officer may not seize an unarmed, nondangerous suspect by shooting him dead. The Tennessee statute is unconstitutional insofar as it authorizes the use of deadly force against such fleeing suspect."

CASE SIGNIFICANCE: This case clarifies the extent to which the police may use deadly force to prevent the escape of an unarmed felon. The Court made it clear that deadly force may be used only if the officer has probable cause to believe that the suspect poses a threat of serious physical harm to the officer or others. In addition, when feasible, the suspect must first be warned. The decision renders unconstitutional existing laws in over half the states that impose no restrictions on the use of force by police officers to prevent the escape of an individual suspected of a felony.

State laws and departmental rules can set narrower limits on the use of force (as in rules stating that use of deadly force may only be used in instance of self-defense), but broader limits are unconstitutional. The court based the decision on the Fourth Amendment, saying that "there can be no question that apprehension by the use of force is a seizure subject to the reasonableness requirement of the Fourth Amendment."

RELATED CASES:
FORD v. CHILDERS, 650 F. Supp. 110 (C.D. Ill., 1986)
GARCIA v. WYCKOFF, 615 F. Supp. 217 (D. COLO., 1985)
GRANDSTAFF v. CITY OF BORGER, 767 F. 2d. 161 (5th Cir. 1985)
RYDER v. CITY OF TOPEKA, 814 F. 2d. 1412 (10th Cir. 1987)

GRAHAM v. CONNOR
109 S. Ct. 1865 (1989)

FACTS: Graham, a diabetic, asked a friend, Berry, to drive him to a convenience store to buy orange juice, which he needed to counteract the onset of an insulin reaction. They went to the store, but Graham saw many people ahead of him in line so he hurried out and asked Berry to drive him, instead, to a friend's house. Officer Connor became suspicious after he saw Graham hastily enter and leave the store. He followed Berry's car, made an investigative stop, and ordered Graham and Berry to wait while he determined what happened at the store. Other officers arrived, handcuffed Graham, and ignored Graham's attempt to explain his condition. An encounter ensued wherein Graham sustained multiple injuries. Graham was later released when officer Connor learned that nothing had happened at the store. Graham brought a Section 1983 lawsuit against the police alleging a violation of his Fourth Amendment constitutional right.

ISSUE: May police officers be held liable under Section 1983 for using excessive force? YES. If yes, what should be the standard for liability?

SUPREME COURT DECISION: Police officers may be held liable under the Constitution for using excessive force. Such liability must be judged under the Fourth Amendment's "objective reasonableness" standard, rather than under a "substantive due process" standard.

REASON: "The 'reasonableness' of a particular use of force must be judged from the perspective of a reasonable officer on the scene, rather than with the 20/20 vision of hindsight. The Fourth Amendment is not violated by an arrest based on probable cause, even though the wrong person is arrested, nor by the mistaken execution of a valid search warrant on the wrong premises. With respect to a claim of excessive force, the same standard of reasonableness at the moment applies: 'Not every push or shove, even if it may later seem unnecessary in the peace of a judge's chamber,' violates the Fourth Amendment. The calculus of reasonableness must embody allowance for the fact that police officers are often forced to make split-second judgements -- in circumstances that are tense, uncertain, and rapidly evolving -- about the amount of force that is necessary in a particular situation." (citations omitted).

CASE SIGNIFICANCE: This case gives police officers a "break" in civil liability cases involving the use of force. The old "substantive due process" test used by many lower courts prior to the *Graham* case required the courts to consider whether the officer acted in "good faith" or "maliciously and sadistically for the very purpose of causing harm." This meant that the officer's "subjective motivations" were of central importance in deciding whether the force used was unconstitutional. The *Graham* case requires a new test, that of "objective reasonableness" under the Fourth Amendment. This means that the reasonableness of an officer's use of force must be judged "from the perspective of a reasonable officer on the scene, rather than with the 20/20 vision of hindsight." This makes a big difference in determining whether or not such use of force was reasonable. This new test recognizes that police officers often make split second judgements in situations that involve their own lives and must, therefore, be judged in the context of "a reasonable officer at the scene." This is a test most police officers welcome.

RELATED CASES:
GRANDSTAFF v. CITY OF BORGER, 767 F. 2d 161 (5th Cir. 1985)
RYDER v. CITY OF TOPEKA, 814 F. 2d 1412 (10th Cir. 1987)
SPRINGFIELD v. KIBBE, 480 U.S. 257 (1987)
TENNESSEE v. GARNER, 471 U.S. 1 (1985)

CONFESSIONS AND ADMISSIONS: CASES SUPPORTING MIRANDA

14

BROWN v. MISSISSIPPI, 297 U.S. 278 (1936)
MIRANDA v. ARIZONA, 384 U.S. 436 (1966)
EDWARDS v. ARIZONA, 451 U.S. 477 (1981)
BERKEMER v. McCARTY, 468 U.S. 420 (1984)
MICHIGAN v. JACKSON, 475 U.S. 625 (1986)
ARIZONA v. ROBERSON, 108 S. Ct. 2093 (1988)

BROWN v. MISSISSIPPI
297 U.S. 278 (1936)

FACTS: A deputy sheriff and others went to Brown's home and requested him to accompany them to the house of the deceased. While there, Brown was accused of the murder. When he denied the accusation, he was hanged from a tree limb, let down, and hanged again. Persisting in his claim of innocence, he was tied to a tree and whipped, but was later released. Several days later, the same deputy returned to Brown's home and arrested him. On the way to the jail, Brown was again beaten by the deputy who said he would continue beating Brown until Brown confessed. Brown did confess and was held in jail.

Two other suspects were taken to the same jail. There they were made to strip by the same deputy and others and were laid over chairs where they were whipped with a leather strap with a buckle on it. When they finally confessed, the officers left, saying that if they changed their story they would be whipped again.

The next day the three were brought before the sheriff and others, at which time they confessed to the crimes. Trial began the next day. The suspects testified that the confessions were false and were obtained by torture. The rope marks on the suspects were clearly visible and none of the participants in the beatings denied they had taken place. The suspects were convicted of murder and sentenced to death.

ISSUE: Are confessions obtained by brutality and torture by law enforcement officers a violation of the due process rights guaranteed by the Fourteenth Amendment? YES.

SUPREME COURT DECISION: Confessions obtained as a result of coercion and brutality by law enforcement officers are violative of the due process clause of the Fourteenth Amendment and are therefore inadmissible in court.

REASON: "The State is free to regulate the procedure of its courts in accordance with its own conceptions of policy, unless in so doing it 'offends some principle of justice so rooted in the traditions and conscience of our people as to be ranked fundamental.'... [T]he freedom of the State in establishing its policy is the freedom of constitutional government and is limited by the requirement of due process of law. Because a State may dispense with a jury trial, it does not follow that it may substitute trial by ordeal. The rack and torture chamber may not be substituted for the witness stand. The State may

not permit an accused to be hurried to conviction under mob domination --
where the whole proceeding is but a mask -- without supplying corrective
process."

CASE SIGNIFICANCE: This case was decided by the Court in 1936, before
the Fifth Amendment right against self-incrimination was made applicable to
the states. Instead of using the Fifth Amendment, the Court used the due
process clause of the Fourteenth Amendment since the Fourteenth Amendment has always been made applicable to state criminal proceedings.

Even before the Fifth Amendment was made applicable to the states,
the Court, through this decision, made it clear that there were state practices
it would not tolerate. *Brown* was a criminal prosecution in a state court
where the suspects were physically tortured to obtain a confession. Such
practice, said the Court, was offensive to the due process clause of the Fourteenth Amendment. This case renders inadmissible in court any evidence
obtained as a result of physical torture. The methods used by the law enforcement officers in *Brown* were extreme, hence it was easy to prohibit their
use. Subsequently, the Court said that any type of physical coercion (not
necessarily hanging, as here) was also prohibited. Still later, even psychological coercion was prohibited. All these culminated in *Miranda v. Arizona* (see
brief in this book) where the test for admissibility shifted from voluntariness
to one of "Were *Miranda* warnings given?" *Brown* represents the first case
where evidence obtained as a result of physical torture in a state court criminal proceeding was held inadmissible by the Supreme Court. If a case similar
to *Brown* were decided today, the evidence would be excluded based on the
exclusionary rule and not on the Fourteenth Amendment Due Process
Clause.

RELATED CASES:
ASHCRAFT v. TENNESSEE, 322 U.S. 143 (1944)
MIRANDA v. ARIZONA, 384 U.S. 436 (1966)
ROGERS v. RICHMOND, 365 U.S. 534 (1961)
TOWNSEND v. SAIN, 372 U.S. 293 (1963)

MIRANDA v. ARIZONA
384 U.S. 436 (1966)

FACTS: Miranda was arrested at his home and taken to a police station for
questioning in connection with a rape and kidnapping. Miranda was 23 years

old, poor, and had completed only half of the ninth grade. The officers interrogated him for two hours, in which time they obtained a written confession. Miranda was convicted of rape and kidnapping.

ISSUE: Must the police inform a suspect who is subject to a custodial interrogation of his or her constitutional rights involving self-incrimination and right to counsel prior to questioning? YES.

SUPREME COURT DECISION: Evidence obtained by the police during custodial interrogation of a suspect cannot be used in court unless the suspect was informed of the following rights prior to the interrogation:
  (1) the right to remain silent;
  (2) that any statement made may be used in a court of law;
  (3) the right to have an attorney present during questioning; and
  (4) if the suspect cannot afford one, one will be appointed for him
       or her prior to questioning.

REASON: "The Fifth Amendment privilege is so fundamental to our system of constitutional rule and the expedient of given an adequate warning as to the availability of the privilege so simple, we will not pause to inquire in individual cases whether the defendant was aware of his rights without a warning being given. Assessments of the knowledge the defendant possessed, based on information as to his age, education, intelligence, or prior contact with authorities, can never be more than speculation; a warning as a clearcut fact. More important, whatever the background of the person interrogated, a warning at the time of the interrogation is indispensable to overcome its pressures and to insure that the individual knows he is free to exercise the privilege at that point in time....The warning of the right to remain silent must be accompanied by the explanation that anything said can and will be used against the individual in court. This warning is needed in order to make him aware not only of the privilege, but also of the consequences of forgoing it. It is only through an awareness of these consequences that there can be any assurance of real understanding and intelligent exercise of the privilege. Moreover, this warning may serve to make the individual more acutely aware that he is faced with a phase of the adversary system -- that he is not in the presence of persons acting solely in his interest."

"The circumstances surrounding in-custody interrogation can operate very quickly to overbear the will of one merely made aware if his privilege by his interrogators. Therefore, the right to have counsel present at interrogation is indispensable to the protection of the Fifth Amendment privilege under the system we delineate today. Our aim is to assure the individual's right to choose between silence and speech remains unfettered throughout the interrogation process...."

"The presence of counsel at the interrogation may serve several significant subsidiary functions as well. If the accused decides to talk to his interrogators, the assistance of counsel can mitigate the dangers of untrustworthiness. With a lawyer present the likelihood that the police will practice coercion is reduced, and if coercion is nevertheless exercised the lawyer can testify to it in court. The presence of a lawyer can also help to guarantee that the accused gives a fully accurate statement to the police and that the statement is rightly reported by the prosecution at trial."

"We have concluded that without proper safeguards the process of in-custody interrogation of persons suspected or accused of crime contains inherently compelling pressures which work to undermine the individual's will to resist and to compel him to speak where he would not otherwise do so freely. In order to combat these pressures and to permit a full opportunity to exercise the privilege against self-incrimination, the accused must be adequately and effectively apprised of his rights and the exercise of those rights must be fully honored."

CASE SIGNIFICANCE: *Miranda v. Arizona* is, arguably, the most widely known case ever to be decided by the U.S. Supreme Court. It also has had the deepest impact on the day-to-day crime investigation phase of police work and has led to changes that have since become an accepted part of routine police procedure. No other law enforcement case has generated more controversy within and outside police circles. Supporters of the *Miranda* decision hail it as properly protective of individual rights, whereas critics have accused the Court of being soft on crime and coddling criminals. The 5-4 split among the justices served to fan the flames of the controversy in its early stages, opponents of the ruling hoping that a change in Court composition would hasten its demise. That has not happened, and neither is it likely to happen in the immediate future. *Miranda* has survived the test of time and, although the process of erosion has begun in recent years, a complete overruling of *Miranda* even by a conservative Court appears remote.

Miranda is unique in that seldom does the Court tell the police exactly what ought to be done. In this case, the court literally told the police what warnings ought to be given if the evidence attained from the interrogation is to be admitted in court. *Miranda* also clarified some of the ambiguous terms used in *Escobedo v. Illinois*, 378 U.S. 428 (1964). "By custodial interrogation," said the Court, "we mean questioning initiated by law enforcement officers after a person has been taken into custody or otherwise deprived of his freedom of action in any significant way." It then added in a footnote: "This is what we meant in *Escobedo* when we spoke of an investigation which had focused on an accused." Yet the "focus" test was abandoned by the Court in later cases, preferring to use the "custodial interrogation" test to determine if the *Miranda* warning needed to be given. The *Escobedo* case brought the right to counsel to the police station prior to trial; the *Miranda* case went beyond the police station and brought the right to counsel out into the street if an interrogation is to take place.

RELATED CASES:
BERKEMER v. McCARTY, 468 U.S. 104 (1984)
FARE v. MICHAEL C., 442 U.S. 707 (1978)
MICHIGAN v. MOSLEY, 423 U.S. 96 (1975)
RHODE ISLAND v. INNIS, 446 U.S. 291 (1980)

EDWARDS v. ARIZONA,
451 U.S. 477 (1981)

FACTS: Edwards was arrested pursuant to a warrant. At the police station, he was read his *Miranda* warnings and indicated that he understood them and would answer questions. After being informed that an accomplice had made a sworn statement implicating him, Edwards sought to "make a deal," but later changed his mind and said that he wanted to speak to an attorney before making a deal. At that point questioning ceased. The next morning, two other officers went to the jail and asked to see Edwards. Edwards told the detention officer that he did not wish to speak to the officers, but was told that he had no choice in the matter. Edwards was again informed of his *Miranda* rights. He indicated that he would talk but first wanted to hear the taped statement of the accomplice. After listening to the statement Edwards made a statement implicating himself in the crime. Edwards was charged with and convicted of several state criminal offenses.

ISSUE: If a suspect has been given the *Miranda* warnings and invokes the right to remain silent or to have counsel, may that suspect be later interrogated by the police if the *Miranda* warnings are given again? NO.

SUPREME COURT DECISION: An accused who, after having been given the *Miranda* warnings, invokes the right to silence and to have a lawyer, cannot be interrogated further by the police until a lawyer has been made available. An exception to this rule is if the accused initiates further communication, exchanges, or conversations with the police.

REASON: "When an accused asks for counsel, a valid waiver of that right cannot be established by showing only that he responded to further police-initiated custodial interrogation even if he has been advised of his rights. We further hold that an accused, such as Edwards, having expressed his desire to deal with the police only through counsel, is not subject to further interrogation by the authorities until counsel has been made available to him, unless the accused himself initiates further communication, exchanges, or conversations with the police."

"We think it clear that Edwards was subjected to custodial interrogation on January 20 within the meaning of *Innis* and that this occurred at the insistence of the authorities. His statement, made without having access to counsel, did not amount to a valid waiver and hence was inadmissible."

CASE SIGNIFICANCE: The principle is clear: once a suspect invokes his or her rights after having been given the *Miranda* warnings, interrogation must cease. Further, the police cannot later interrogate the suspect again, even with another reading of the *Miranda* warnings, until the suspect has been provided a lawyer. If the suspect, however, on his or her own, initiates further communication or conversation with the police, the confession will be admissible. In such instances, there is a need for the suspect to be given the *Miranda* warnings again.

RELATED CASES:
BREWER v. WILLIAMS, 430 U.S. 387 (1977)
MICHIGAN v. MOSLEY, 423 U.S. 96 (1975)
MIRANDA v. ARIZONA, 384 U.S. 436 (1966)
NORTH CAROLINA v. BUTLER, 441 U.S. 369 (1979)

BERKEMER v. McCARTY
468 U.S. 420 (1984)

FACTS: After following McCarty's car for two miles and observing it weave in and out of a lane, an officer stopped the car and asked McCarty to get out of the vehicle. McCarty had difficulty standing while getting out of the car. The officer decided that McCarty would be charged with a traffic offense, thus terminating his freedom to leave the scene. McCarty was not told he would be taken into custody but was required to take a field sobriety test, which he failed. While still at the scene of the stop, McCarty was asked if he had been using any intoxicants, to which he replied that he had consumed two beers and several marijuana cigarettes. McCarty was then formally arrested and taken to jail. A test given to McCarty to determine his blood-alcohol level did not detect any alcohol. The officer resumed the questioning in which McCarty admitted to consuming alcohol. At no point was McCarty given his *Miranda* warnings. McCarty plead no contest and was found guilty of operating a motor vehicle while under the influence of alcohol and/or drugs.

ISSUE:
1. Must the *Miranda* [*v. Arizona*, 384 U.S. 436 (1966)] warnings be given when interrogating suspects charged with misdemeanor traffic offenses? YES.
2. Does the roadside questioning of a motorist detained for a traffic violation constitute a custodial interrogation under *Miranda v. Arizona*? NO.

SUPREME COURT DECISION:
1. A person subjected to custodial interrogation must be given *Miranda* warnings regardless of the nature or severity of the offense.
2. The roadside questioning of a motorist detained pursuant to a routine traffic stop does not constitute a custodial interrogation, hence no *Miranda* warnings need be given.

REASON: "In the years since the decision in *Miranda*, we have frequently reaffirmed the central principle established by that case: if the police take a suspect into custody and then ask him questions without informing him of the rights enumerated above, his responses cannot be introduced into evidence to establish his guilt...."

"Petitioner asks us to carve an exception out of the foregoing principle. When the police arrest a person for allegedly committing a misdemeanor traffic offense and then ask him questions without telling him his constitutional rights, petitioners argue, his responses should be admissible against him. We cannot agree."

"One of the principal advantages of the doctrine that suspects must be given warnings before being interrogateed while in custody is the clarity of that rule....The exception to *Miranda* proposed by petitioner would substantially undermine this crucial advantage of the doctrine. The police often are unaware when they arrest a person whether he may have committed a misdemeanor or a felony...."

"Two features of an ordinary traffic stop mitigate the danger that a person questioned will be induced 'to speak where he would not otherwise do so freely.' *Miranda v. Arizona*, 384 U.S. at 476. First, detention of a motorist pursuant to a traffic stop is presumably temporary and brief. The vast majority of roadside detentions last only a few minutes.... Second, circumstances associated with the typical traffic stop are not such that the motorist feels completely at the mercy of the police."

CASE SIGNIFICANCE: This case settles two legal issues that had long divided lower courts. It is clear now that once a suspect has been placed under arrest for any offense, be it felony or misdemeanor, the *Miranda* warnings must be given before interrogation. It is a rule that is easier for the police to follow than the requirement of determining if the arrest was for a felony or a misdemeanor before giving the warning. The Court said that the purpose of the *Miranda* warnings, which is to ensure that the police do not coerce or trick captive suspects into confessing, is applicable equally to misdemeanor or felony cases. The second part of the decision is equally important in that it identifies an instance when the warnings need not be given. There is no custodial interrogation in a traffic stop because it is usually brief and the motorist expects that, although he or she may be given a citation, in the end the motorist will most likely be allowed to continue on his or her way. However, if the motorist who has been temporarily detained is later arrested, the *Miranda* warnings must be given if interrogation is to take place.

RELATED CASES:
MATHIS v. UNITED STATES, 391 U.S. 1 (1968)
MINNESOTA v. MURPHY, 465 U.S. 420 (1984)
MIRANDA v. ARIZONA, 384 U.S. 436 (1966)
TERRY v. OHIO, 392 U.S. 1 (1968)

MICHIGAN v. JACKSON
475 U.S. 625 (1986)

FACTS: Jackson was one of four participants in a wife's plan to have her husband killed. When arrested on an unrelated charge, he made a series of statements during a police interrogation prior to his arraignment. At arraignment, Jackson requested the assistance of counsel and one was appointed for him. The following morning, before Jackson had a chance to consult with counsel, officers obtained another statement confirming that he was the murderer. All of the statements were given after Jackson was advised of his *Miranda* rights and agreed to talk without the presence of counsel. Jackson was charged with and convicted of second-degree murder and conspiracy to commit second-degree murder.

ISSUE: May an accused who has requested the assistance of counsel during arraignment waive that right at police-initiated post-arraignment custodial interrogations? NO.

SUPREME COURT DECISION: If the police initiate an interrogation after the defendant asserts his or her right to counsel at arraignment or similar proceedings, any waiver of that right for a police-initiated interrogation is invalid.

REASON: "Although the rule of *Edwards v. Arizona*, 451 U.S. 477 [1981], that once a suspect has invoked his right to counsel, police may not initiate interrogation until counsel has been made available to the suspect, rested on the Fifth Amendment and concerned a request for counsel made during custodial interrogation, the reasoning of that case applies with even greater force to this case. The assertion of the right to counsel is no less significant, and the need for additional safeguards no less clear, when that assertion is made at arraignment and when the basis for it is the Sixth Amendment. If police initiate an interrogation after defendant's assertion of his right to counsel, at an arraignment or similar proceeding, as in this case, any waiver of that right for that police initiated interrogation is invalid."

CASE SIGNIFICANCE: The rule is clear that if a suspect invokes his or her right to remain silent, the police should not and cannot initiate interrogation with the suspect. This rule does not apply if the suspect initiates the conversation on his or her own. If the police violate this rule, the admission or confession obtained will not be admissible in court. The situation in the *Jackson* case is different in that the defendant here invoked the right to counsel at arraignment (when the charges are read to the accused in court), not during police interrogation. What was also invoked was not the right to remain silent, but the right to a lawyer. Nonetheless, the Court said that after the accused requested counsel during arraignment, the police should no longer interrogate him, even with the *Miranda* warnings, if the accused has not yet conferred with a lawyer. The rule is clear: Once an accused asks for or has a lawyer, the police must not interrogate the accused except in the presence of a lawyer.

RELATED CASES:
EDWARDS v. ARIZONA, 451 U.S. 477 (1981)
McLEOD v. OHIO, 381 U.S. 356 (1965)
MAINE v. MOULTON, 474 U.S. 159 (1985)
SOLEM v. STUMES, 465 U.S. 638 (1984)

ARIZONA v. ROBERSON
486 U.S. 675 (1988)

FACTS: After being arrested at the scene of a burglary, Roberson was advised of his *Miranda* rights and indicated that he wanted to speak to a lawyer before answering any questions. Three days later, a different officer, unaware of Roberson's request for counsel, gave him the *Miranda* warnings and interrogated him concerning a different burglary. Roberson made incriminating statements concerning the crime.

ISSUE: If an accused has invoked the right to counsel, may the police, after given the *Miranda* warnings again, interrogate the same suspect about a different crime? NO.

SUPREME COURT DECISION: An accused who has invoked the right to counsel, may not be subjected to a police-initiated interrogation even if the interrogation concerns a different crime.

REASON: "The *Edwards* rule applies to bar police-initiated interrogation following a suspect's request for counsel in the context of a separate investigation."

"The bright-line prophylactic *Edwards* rule benefits the accused and the State alike. It protects against the inherently compelling pressures of custodial interrogation [on] suspects who feel incapable of undergoing such questioning without the advice of counsel, by creating a presumption that any subsequent waiver of the right to counsel at the authorities' behest was coercive and not purely voluntary. Moreover, it provides clear and unequivocal guidelines that inform police and prosecutors with specificity what they may do in conducting custodial interrogation, and that inform courts under what circumstances statements obtained during interrogation are not admissible."

CASE SIGNIFICANCE: An earlier case, *Edwards v. Arizona*, 451 U.S. 477 (1980), said that if an accused asks for counsel after having been given the *Miranda* warnings, that accused cannot be further interrogated by the police. This case differs from *Edwards* in that:
  (1) the second interrogation took place three days later (instead of the day after, as in Edwards); and
  (2) the interrogation was for a different offense.

Nonetheless, the Court said that the rule is the same, an accused who had invoked the right to counsel may not be subjected to police interrogation again, even if it be for a different offense. Although the Court did not explicitly say so, it is to be assumed that the exception in *Edwards*, where interrogations are allowed if the suspect initiates the communication or conversation, also applies to interrogations for a different offense.

RELATED CASES:
COLORADO v. SPRING, 479 U.S. 564 (1987)
EDWARDS v. ARIZONA, 451 U.S. 477 (1981)
MICHIGAN v. MOSLEY, 423 U.S. 96 (1975)
SMITH v. ILLINOIS, 469 U.S. 91 (1984)

CONFESSIONS AND ADMISSIONS: CASES ERODING MIRANDA

15

SOUTH DAKOTA v. NEVILLE, 459 U.S. 553 (1983)
NEW YORK v. QUARLES, 467 U.S. 649 (1984)
OREGON v. ELSTAD, 470 U.S. 298 (1985)
COLORADO v. CONNELLY, 479 U.S. 157 (1986)
COLORADO v. SPRING, 479 U.S. 564 (1987)
CONNECTICUT v. BARRETT, 479 U.S. 523 (1987)
DUCKWORTH v. EAGAN, 109 S. Ct. 2875 (1989)
PATTERSON v. ILLINOIS, 487 U.S. 285 (1988)

SOUTH DAKOTA v. NEVILLE
459 U.S. 553 (1983)

FACTS: South Dakota law permits a person suspected of driving while intoxicated to submit to a blood-alcohol test and authorizes revocation of the driver's license of any person who refuses to take the test. The statute permits such refusal to be used against the driver as evidence of guilt during the trial. Neville was arrested by the police for driving while intoxicated. He was asked to submit to a blood-alcohol test and warned that he could lose his license if he refused to take the test. He was not warned, however, that the refusal could be used against him during trial. Neville refused to take the test. During trial, Neville sought to exclude the evidence obtained, claiming that it violated his right to protection against compulsory self-incrimination.

ISSUE: Does a state law that allows the admission into evidence of a suspect's refusal to submit to a blood-alcohol test violate the suspect's Fifth Amendment right against self-incrimination? NO.

SUPREME COURT DECISION: The admission into evidence of a defendant's refusal to submit to a blood-alcohol test does not violate the suspect's Fifth Amendment right against self-incrimination. A refusal to take such a test, after a police officer has lawfully requested it, is not an act coerced by the officer, and thus is not protected by the Fifth Amendment. A law that allows the accused to refuse to take a blood alcohol test and provides that such refusal may be admitted in evidence against him or her is constitutional.

REASON: "The simple blood-alcohol test is so safe, painless, and commonplace that respondent concedes, as he must, that the state could legitimately compel the suspect, against his will, to accede to the test. Given, then, that the offer of taking a blood-alcohol test is clearly legitimate, the action becomes no less legitimate when the State offers a second option of refusing the test, with the attendant penalties for making that choice. Nor is this a case where the State has subtly coerced respondent into choosing the option it had no right to compel, rather than offering a true choice. To the contrary, the State wants respondent to choose to take the test, for the inference of intoxication arising from a positive blood-alcohol test is far stronger than that arising from a refusal to take the test.... We recognize, of course, that the choice to submit or refuse to take a blood-alcohol test will not be an easy or pleasant one for a suspect to make. But the criminal process often requires suspects and defendants to make difficult choices. We hold, therefore, that a refusal to take a blood-alcohol test, after a police officer has lawfully requested it, is not an act coerced by the officer, and thus is not protected by the privilege against self-incrimination."

CASE SIGNIFICANCE: This case legitimizes the practice, established by law in many states, of giving suspected DWI offenders a choice to take or refuse blood-alcohol tests but to use the refusal as evidence of guilt later in court. The defendant in this case argued that introducing such evidence in court, in effect, coerces the suspect to waive constitutional protection against self-incrimination because of the consequence. The Court rejected this contention, saying that any incrimination resulting from a blood-alcohol test is physical in nature, not testimonial, and hence is not protected by the Fifth Amendment. Therefore, a suspect has no constitutional right to refuse to take the test. The Court said that the offer to the suspect to take the test is clearly legitimate and becomes no less legitimate when the state offers the option of refusing the test but prescribes consequences for making that choice. The Court added that the failure by the police to warn Neville that his refusal to take the test could be used as evidence against him during the trial was not so fundamentally unfair as to deprive him of "due process" rights. The evidence obtained could, therefore be admissible during trial.

RELATED CASES:
GILBERT v. CALIFORNIA, 388 U.S. 263 (1967)
ROCHIN v. CALIFORNIA, 342 U.S. 165 (1952)
STOVAL v. DENNO, 388 U.S. 293 (1967)
UNITED STATES v. WADE, 388 U.S. 318 (1967)

NEW YORK v. QUARLES
467 U.S. 649 (1984)

FACTS: Officers were approached by a woman claiming that she had just been raped by an armed man. She described him, and said that he had entered a nearby supermarket. The officers drove the woman to the supermarket and one officer went in while the other radioed for assistance. The officer in the supermarket quickly spotted Quarles, who matched the description provided by the woman, and a chase ensued. The officer ordered Quarles to stop and place his hands over his head. The officer frisked Quarles and discovered an empty shoulder holster. After handcuffing Quarles, the officer asked him where the gun was. Quarles nodded in the direction of some empty cartons and responded, "the gun is over there." The gun was retrieved from the cartons and Quarles was placed under arrest and read his *Miranda* warnings. Quarles indicated that he would answer questions without an attorney present and admitted that he owned the gun.

ISSUE: Were the suspect's initial statements and the gun admissible in evidence despite the failure of the officer to give him the *Miranda* warnings prior to asking questions that led to the discovery of the gun? YES.

SUPREME COURT DECISION: Responses to questions asked by a police officer which are reasonably prompted by concern for public safety are admissible in court even though the suspect was in police custody and was not given the *Miranda* warnings.

REASON: "We hold that on these facts there is a 'public safety' exception to the requirement that *Miranda* warnings be given before a suspect's answers may be admitted into evidence, and that the availability of that exception does not depend upon the motivation of the individual officers involved. In a kaleidoscopic situation such as the one confronting these officers, where spontaneity rather than adherence to a police manual is necessarily the order of the day, the application of the exception which we recognize today should not be made to depend on *post hoc* findings at a suppression hearing concerning the subjective motivation of the arresting officer. Undoubtedly most police officers, if placed in Officer Kraft's position, would act out of a host of different, instinctive, and largely unverifiable motives -- their own safety, the safety of others, and perhaps as well the desire to obtain incriminating evidence from the suspect."

CASE SIGNIFICANCE: *New York v. Quarles* carves out a "public safety" exception to the *Miranda* rule. The Court said that the case presents a situation in which concern for public safety must be paramount to adherence to the literal language of the rules enunciated in *Miranda*. Here, although Quarles was in police custody and therefore should have been given the *Miranda* warnings, concern for public safety prevailed. In this case, said the Court, the gun was concealed somewhere in the supermarket and, therefore, posed more than one danger to the public. The Court hinted, however, that the "public safety" exception needs to be interpreted narrowly and added that police officers can and will distinguish almost instinctively between questions necessary to secure their own safety or the safety of the public and questions designed solely to elicit testimony evidence from a suspect. Whether or not the police will be able to do this remains to be seen.

RELATED CASES:
BERKEMER v. McCARTY, 468 U.S. 420 (1984)
MIRANDA v. ARIZONA, 384 U.S. 436 (1966)
OREGON v. MATHIASON, 429 U.S. 492 (1977)
OROZCO v. TEXAS, 394 U.S. 324 (1969)

OREGON v. ELSTAD
470 U.S. 298 (1985)

FACTS: Officers went to a burglary suspect's home with a warrant for his arrest. Elstad's mother answered the door and led the officers to her son's room. One officer waited with Elstad while the other explained his arrest to the mother. The officer told Elstad that he was implicated in the burglary, to which he responded "Yes, I was there." Elstad was then taken to the police station where he was advised of his *Miranda* rights for the first time. Elstad indicated that he understood his rights and wanted to talk to the officers. He then made a full statement which was typed, reviewed and read back to Elstad for corrections, then signed by the officer and Elstad. Elstad was charged with and convicted of first-degree burglary.

ISSUE: Do voluntary but unwarned statements made prior to *Miranda* warnings render all subsequent statements inadmissible under the Fifth Amendment's protection from self-incrimination? NO.

SUPREME COURT DECISION: If a confession is made after proper *Miranda* warnings and waiver of rights, the Fifth Amendment does not make it inadmissible solely because the police obtained an earlier voluntary but unwarned admission from the suspect.

REASON: "Far from establishing a rigid rule, we direct courts to avoid one; there is no warrant for presuming coercive effect where the suspect's initial inculpatory statement, though technically in violation of *Miranda*, was voluntary. The relevant inquiry is whether, in fact, the second statement was also made voluntarily. As in any such inquiry, the finder of fact must examine the surrounding circumstances and the entire course of police conduct with respect to the suspect in evaluating the voluntariness of his statements. The fact that a suspect chooses to speak after being informed of his rights is, of course, highly probative. We find that the dictates of *Miranda* and the goals of the Fifth Amendment proscription against use of compelled testimony are fully satisfied in the circumstances of this case by barring the use of the unwarned statement in the case in chief. No further purpose is served by imputing 'taint' to subsequent statements obtained pursuant to a voluntary and knowing waiver."

CASE SIGNIFICANCE: This case partly erodes the *Miranda* doctrine by holding that "a suspect who has once responded to unwarned yet uncoercive questioning is not thereby disabled from waiving his or her rights and confessing after he or she has been given the requisite *Miranda* warnings." The suspect in this case alleged that the "statement he made in response to questioning at his house (without *Miranda* warnings) 'let the cat out of the bag,'... and tainted the subsequent confessions as 'fruit of the poisonous tree.'" In most cases, the courts have held that any evidence obtained as a result of an illegal act by the police is inadmissible in court because it is, indeed, fruit of the poisonous tree. Such was not the case here, however, because, while the statement, "Yes I was there," from Elstad was inadmissible because it was in response to a police question asked before the *Miranda* warnings were given, such an act by the police was not, in itself, illegal. As long as subsequent facts prove that the second statement, after *Miranda* warnings were given, was valid, the fact that no warnings were given earlier does not render the second statement inadmissible. The police should note, however, that the rule still holds that if the police commit an illegal act, any evidence obtained as a result of that illegal act is inadmissible as "fruit of the poisonous tree."

RELATED CASES:
BECKWITH v. UNITED STATES, 425 U.S. 341 (1976)
HAYNES v. WASHINGTON, 373 U.S. 503 (1963)
MICHIGAN v. TUCKER, 417 U.S. 433 (1974)
MIRANDA v. ARIZONA, 384 U.S. 436 (1966)

COLORADO v. CONNELLY
479 U.S. 157 (1986)

FACTS: Connelly approached a uniformed Denver police officer and confessed that he had murdered someone in Denver in 1982 and wanted to talk to the officer about it. The officer advised Connelly of his *Miranda* rights. Connelly indicated that he understood his rights and wanted to talk about the murder. After a homicide detective arrived, Connelly was again advised of his *Miranda* rights and again indicated that he understood them and still wanted to speak with the police. Connelly was then taken to the police station where he told officers that he had come from Boston to confess to the murder. He made a full statement of the facts, and agreed to take the officers to the scene of the murder. When he became visibly disoriented, he was sent to a state hospital where, in an interview with a psychiatrist, Connelly revealed that he was following the advice of God in confessing to the murder. He was found incompetent to assist in his own defense but competent to stand trial.

ISSUE: Is a suspect's waiver of the *Miranda* rights that is not fully rational (because he was allegedly "following the advice of God") valid? YES.

SUPREME COURT DECISION: The admissibility of statements made when the mental state of the defendant interfered with his "rational intellect" and "free will" is governed by state rules of evidence rather than previous Supreme Court decisions regarding coerced confessions and the *Miranda* waivers. Such evidence therefore is not automatically excluded; its admissibility instead depends upon state rules.

REASON: "We have...observed that 'jurists and scholars have recognized that the exclusionary rule imposes a substantial cost on the societal interest in law enforcement by its proscription of what concededly is relevant evidence.' ...Moreover, suppressing respondent's statements would serve absolutely no purpose in enforcing constitutional guarantees. The purpose of excluding evidence seized in violation of the Constitution is to substantially deter future violations of the Constitution.... Only if we were to establish a brand new constitutional right -- the right of a criminal defendant to confess to his crime only when totally rational and properly motivated -- could respondent's present claim be sustained."

CASE SIGNIFICANCE: The Court indicated in this case that confessions and admissions are involuntary and invalid under the Constitution, only if coercive police activity is involved. If the waiver is caused by anything other than police behavior, admissibility of the confession should depend on the state's rules of evidence. It is clear in this case that the *Miranda* warnings were repeatedly given and that there was a waiver. Such waiver, however, was later challenged as involuntary because it was promoted by a "voice of God." The Court said that this was not sufficient to render the waiver involuntary because the police did not act improperly or illegally. As long as police behavior is legal, a waiver is considered voluntary under the Constitution and its admissibility is governed by state law. This means that if state law allows its admissibility, such evidence can be used.

RELATED CASES:
BLACKBURN v. ALABAMA, 361 U.S. 199 (1960)
MORAN v. BURBINE, 475 U.S. 412 (1986)
TOWNSEND v. SAIN, 372 U.S. 293 (1963)
SPANO v. NEW YORK, 360 U.S. 315 (1959)

COLORADO v. SPRING
479 U.S. 564 (1987)

FACTS: Spring and a companion shot a man during a hunting trip in Denver. An informant told federal agents that Spring was engaged in interstate trafficking in stolen firearms and that he had participated in the murder. Pursuant to that information, agents set up an undercover operation and arrested Spring in Kansas City. Agents advised Spring of his *Miranda* rights upon arrest. At the agent's office, Spring was again advised of his *Miranda* rights and signed a statement that he understood and waived his rights. Agents then asked Spring about his involvement in the firearms transactions leading to his arrest. He was also asked if he had ever shot a man, to which he responded affirmatively, but denied the shooting in question. Thereafter, Colorado officials questioned Spring. He was again read his *Miranda* warnings and again signed a statement asserting that he understood and waived his rights. This time, Spring confessed to the Colorado murder. A written statement of his confession was prepared which Spring read, edited, and signed. Spring was charged with and convicted of first-degree murder.

ISSUE: Must a suspect be informed of all crimes of which he or she is to be questioned before there can be a valid waiver of the Fifth Amendment privilege against self-incrimination? NO.

SUPREME COURT DECISION: A suspect's waiver of *Miranda* rights is valid even if he or she believes the interrogation will focus on minor crimes but the police shift the questioning to cover a different and more serious crime.

REASON: "Respondent's March 30 decision to waive his Fifth Amendment privilege was voluntary absent evidence that his will was overborne and his capacity for self-determination critically impaired because of coercive police conduct. His waiver was also knowingly and intelligently made, that is, he understood that he had the right to remain silent and that anything he said could be used as evidence against him. The constitution does not require that a suspect know and understand every possible consequence of a waiver of the Fifth Amendment privilege. Here, there was no allegation that respondent failed to understand that privilege or that he misunderstood the consequences of speaking freely."

CASE SIGNIFICANCE: The confession was held valid in this case because there was no deception or misrepresentation by the police in obtaining the confession. Here, the police first questioned Spring about firearms transactions (a lesser offense) and, after he incriminated himself on these, the police asked him about a more serious offense, the murder, where Spring again incriminated himself. Spring, in challenging the validity of the waiver, felt that he ought to have been informed first of the offense for which he would be interrogated. The Court said that the police did not have to do so as long as there was no intention on the part of the police to mislead or deceive Spring. The principle is that a valid waiver of the *Miranda* rights allows the police to ask questions of the suspect about any crime as long as such interrogation does not involve misrepresentation or deception. There is no need to repeat the *Miranda* warnings again if the suspect is asked about a different crime.

RELATED CASES:
MICHIGAN v. TUCKER, 417 U.S. 433 (1974)
MIRANDA v. ARIZONA, 384 U.S. 436 (1966)
MORAN v. BURBINE, 475 U.S. 412 (1986)
OREGON v. ELSTAD, 470 U.S. 298 (1985)

CONNECTICUT v. BARRETT
479 U.S. 523 (1987)

FACTS: Barrett was arrested in connection with a sexual assault. Upon arrival at the police station Barrett was advised of his *Miranda* rights and signed a statement acknowledging the understanding of his rights. Barrett stated that he would not give a written statement in the absence of counsel but that he would talk to the police about the incident. In two subsequent interrogations, Barrett was again advised of his rights and signed a statement of understanding. On both occasions he gave an oral statement admitting his involvement in the assault but refused to make a written statement. Because of a malfunction in the tape recorder, an officer reduced the confession to writing based on his recollection of the conversation. Barrett was charged with and convicted of sexual assault.

ISSUE: Is there a valid waiver of the *Miranda* rights if a defendant requests assistance of counsel and refuses to make written statements but makes oral statements voluntarily to the police? YES.

SUPREME COURT DECISION: The oral confession made by a suspect is admissible as evidence in court even if the suspect tells the police he would talk with them but would not make a written statement without a lawyer present. The waiver of *Miranda* rights by Barrett is valid because he was not "threatened, tricked, or cajoled" into speaking to the police.

REASON: "Respondent's statements to the police made it clear his willingness to talk about the sexual assault, and, there being no evidence that he was 'threatened, tricked, or cajoled' into speaking to the police, the trial court properly found that his decision to do so constituted a voluntary waiver of his right to counsel. Although the *Miranda* rules were designed to protect defendant from being compelled by the government to make statements, they also gave defendants the right to choose between speech and silence."

"Respondent's invocation of his right to counsel was limited by its terms to the making of written statements, and did not prohibit all further discussions with the police. Requests for counsel must be given broad, all-inclusive effect only when the defendant's words, understood as ordinary people would understand them, are ambiguous. Here, respondent clearly and unequivocally expressed his willingness to speak to police after the sexual assault."

CASE SIGNIFICANCE: The issue in this case was the validity of the waiver of *Miranda* rights. The defendant told the police he would talk with them but would not make a written statement without a lawyer present. Ordinarily, a waiver is unconditional; here, the waiver was conditional in that the suspect did agree to make oral statements without a lawyer present. He later challenged his incriminating oral statements as inadmissible because he had asked for a lawyer, even though he agreed to make an oral statement. The Court rejected the challenge, saying that the sole test for the admissibility of an oral confession was voluntariness. There was a voluntary waiver of rights here although defendant refused to make a written statement. What this case tells the police is that the waiver of rights does not have to be complete or unconditional to be valid. Refusal to have a statement in writing does not make an admission or confession inadmissible, as long as the police can establish that the *Miranda* warnings were given and the waiver was intelligent and voluntary.

RELATED CASES:
ARIZONA v. MAURO, 481 U.S. 520 (1986)
EDWARDS v. ARIZONA, 451 U.S. 477 (1981)
MIRANDA v. ARIZONA, 384 U.S. 436 (1966)
OREGON v. BRADSHAW, 462 U.S. 1039 (1983)

DUCKWORTH v. EAGAN
109 S. Ct. 2875 (1989)

FACTS: Duckworth, when first questioned by Indiana police in connection with a stabbing, made exculpatory statements after having signed a waiver form that provided, among other things, that if he could not afford a lawyer, one would be appointed for him "if and when you go to court." Twenty-nine hours later, he was interviewed again and signed a different waiver form. He confessed to the stabbing and led officers to a site where they recovered relevant physical evidence. Over respondent's objection, his two statements were admitted into evidence at trial. Duckworth was charged with and convicted of attempted murder. He challenged his confession as inadmissible, saying that the first waiver form did not comply with the requirements of *Miranda*; therefore, his confessions were not admissible.

ISSUE: Was the waiver form used by the police in this case (which informed the suspect that an attorney would be appointed for him "if and when you go to court") sufficient to comply with the requirements of *Miranda v. Arizona*? YES.

SUPREME COURT DECISION: The *Miranda* warnings need not be given in the exact form as outlined in the case; they must simply convey to the suspect his or her rights. The initial warning given to Duckworth in this case, namely: the right to remain silent, that anything said could be used against him in court, that he had the right to talk to a lawyer for advice before and during questioning even if he could not afford to hire one, that he had the right to stop answering questions at any time until he talked to a lawyer, and that the police could not provide him with a lawyer, but one would be appointed for him, "if and when you go to court," complied with all the requirements of the *Miranda* case. The evidence obtained was, therefore, admissible.

REASON: "We think it must be relatively commonplace for a suspect, after receiving *Miranda* warnings, to ask *when* he will obtain counsel. The 'if and when you go to court' advice simply anticipates the question. Second, *Miranda* does not require that attorneys be producible on call, but only that the suspect be informed, as here, that he has the right to an attorney before and during questioning, and that an attorney would be appointed for him if he could not afford one. The Court in *Miranda* emphasized that it was not suggesting that 'each police station must have a "stationhouse lawyer" present at all times to advise prisoners.' If the police cannot provide appointed counsel, *Miranda* requires only that the police not question a suspect unless he waives his right to counsel. Here, respondent did just that."

CASE SIGNIFICANCE: This case clarifies two unclear points in the *Miranda* case. First, must the police use the exact wording in the *Miranda* decision to warn a suspect of his or her rights? The Court said no. It is sufficient that the warnings, however worded, "reasonably convey to a suspect his rights." Note, however, that although the warnings need not be adopted verbatim from the *Miranda* case, the substance of the warnings, as indicated above, must be conveyed to the suspect. The second point addresses whether the police must immediately produce a lawyer if a suspect asks for one. The Court also said no. There is no requirement that the police produce a lawyer on call. The police need to inform the suspect the he or she has a right to an attorney and to an appointed attorney if the suspect cannot afford one. If the suspect wants a lawyer and the police cannot immediately provide one, the interrogation simply stops; there is no obligation to provide a lawyer immediately. If the interrogation continues, however, any evidence obtained cannot be used in court.

RELATED CASES:
BREWER v. WILLIAMS, 430 U.S. 387 (1977)
CALIFORNIA v. PRYSOCK, 453 U.S. 355 (1981)
ESCOBEDO v. ILLINOIS, 378 U.S. 478 (1964)
MIRANDA v. ARIZONA, 384 U.S. 436 (1966)

PATTERSON v. ILLINOIS
487 U.S. 285 (1988)

FACTS: After being informed by the police that he had been charged with murder, Patterson, who was in police custody, twice indicated his willingness to discuss the crime with the authorities.   He was interviewed twice and, on both occasions, was read a form waiving his *Miranda* rights.   He initialed each of the five specific warnings on the form and then signed it.   He then gave incriminating statements to the police about his participation in the crime.   He was tried and convicted of murder.

ISSUE: Is a waiver of rights after the *Miranda* warnings a waiver of the Sixth Amendment right to counsel as well as a waiver of the Fifth Amendment right against self-incrimination?   YES.

SUPREME COURT DECISION: A defendant who has been given the *Miranda* warnings has been sufficiently made aware of the Sixth Amendment right to counsel so that any waiver of that right is valid if it is a knowing and intelligent waiver.

REASON: "This Court has never adopted petitioner's suggestion that the Sixth Amendment right to counsel is 'superior' to or 'more difficult' to waive than its Fifth Amendment counterpart.   Rather, in Sixth Amendment cases, the court has defined the scope of the right to counsel by a pragmatic assessment of the usefulness of counsel to the accused at the particular stage of the proceedings in question, and the dangers to the accused of proceedings without counsel at that stage.... *Miranda* warnings are sufficient for this purpose in post-indictment questioning context, because, at that stage, the role of counsel is relatively simple and limited, and the dangers and disadvantages of self-representation are less substantial and more obvious to an accused that they are at trial."

CASE SIGNIFICANCE: Many police officers believe that *Miranda v. Arizona* is a right-to-counsel case.   It is not.   Instead, it is a right against self-incrimination case, meaning that the main reason *Miranda* warnings must be given by the police is that these warnings protect a suspect's right against self-incrimination.   The statement that "you have the right to a lawyer" is given primarily because a lawyer can help protect a suspect's self-incrimination privilege.   In this case, Patterson conceded that he validly waived his Fifth

Amendment right when he signed the waiver, but asserted that such waiver did not mean a waiver of his Sixth Amendment right to counsel, a right given the accused after charges are filed, as they were in this case. In essence, Patterson maintained that he ought to have been specifically informed of his right to counsel (apart from the *Miranda* warnings) and that there must be a separate waiver for that right. The Court disagreed, saying that the *Miranda* warnings were sufficient to inform Patterson of both rights and that his statements were, therefore, admissible in evidence.

RELATED CASES:
BREWER v. WILLIAMS, 430 U.S. 387 (1977)
EDWARDS v. ARIZONA, 451 U.S. 477 (1981)
MICHIGAN v. JACKSON, 475 U.S. 625 (1986)
NORTH CAROLINA v. BUTLER, 441 U.S. 369 (1979)

WHAT CONSTITUTES
INTERROGATION?

16

BREWER v. WILLIAMS, 430 U.S. 387 (1977)
RHODE ISLAND v. INNIS, 446 U.S. 291 (1980)
ARIZONA v. MAURO, 481 U.S. 520 (1987)

BREWER v. WILLIAMS
430 U.S. 387 (1977)

FACTS: The day before Christmas, a ten-year-old girl disappeared from a YMCA building in Des Moines, Iowa. A short time later Williams, an escapee from a mental hospital and a religious person, was seen leaving the YMCA with a large bundle wrapped in a blanket. A 14-year-old boy who helped him reported that he had seen "two legs in it and they were skinny and white." Williams's car was found the next day 160 miles east of Des Moines. Items of clothing belonging to the missing child and a blanket like the one used to wrap the bundle were found at a rest stop between the YMCA in Des Moines and Davenport, where the car was found. Assuming that the girl's body could be found between the YMCA and the car, a massive search was conducted. Meanwhile, Williams was arrested by police in Davenport and was arraigned. Williams's counsel was informed by the police that Williams would be returned to Des Moines without being interrogated by the police. During the trip an officer began a conversation with Williams in which he said that the girl ought to be given a Christian burial before a snowstorm, which might prevent the body from being found. As Williams and the officer neared the town where the body was hidden, Williams agreed to take the officer to the child's body. The body was found about two miles from one of the search teams. At the trial, a motion to suppress the evidence was denied and Williams was convicted of first-degree murder.

ISSUE: Was what the police did in talking to Williams about a "Christian burial" equivalent to interrogating a suspect without giving him his right to counsel? YES.

SUPREME COURT DECISION: Interrogation takes place not only when direct questions are asked but also when, as in this case, the police officers, knowing the defendant's religious interest, make remarks designed to appeal to that interest and therefore induce a confession. In this case, the police officer's "Christian burial" speech was equivalent to an interrogation; therefore, Williams was entitled to the assistance of counsel at that time.

REASON: "There can be no serious doubt...that Detective Leaming deliberately and designedly set out to elicit information from Williams just as surely as -- and perhaps more effectively than -- if he had formally interrogated him. Detective Leaming was fully aware before departing from Des Moines that Williams was being represented in Davenport by [lawyer] Kelly and in Des Moines by [lawyer] McKnight. Yet he purposely sought during Williams's isolation from his lawyers to obtain as much information as possible. Indeed Detective Leaming conceded as much when he testified at Williams's trial."

CASE SIGNIFICANCE: There are two important principles for the police in this case. The first is that once a suspect has been formally charged with an offense and has a lawyer, he or she should not be interrogated unless there is a valid waiver. The second is that conversations with or appeals to the suspect that may induce a confession constitute an interrogation that then requires both *Miranda* warnings and the right to counsel.

This case declares that "interrogation" by the police does not simply mean asking direct questions. In this case, the police had been told by the lawyers for the suspect that he was not to be interrogated while being transported from Davenport to Des Moines. The police assured the lawyers that Williams would not be interrogated. There was, in fact, no interrogation, but the police officer gave Williams what became known as the "Christian burial speech" wherein he addressed Williams as "Reverend" and pleaded that "the parents of this little girl should be entitled to a Christian burial for the little girl who was snatched away from them on Christmas Eve and murdered." The Court said that the speech was the functional equivalent of an interrogation and therefore violated the suspect's right to counsel.

RELATED CASES:
ESCOBEDO v. ILLINOIS, 378 U.S. 478 (1964)
MASSIAH v. UNITED STATES, 377 U.S. 201 (1964)
MIRANDA v. ARIZONA, 384 U.S. 436 (1966)
RHODE ISLAND v. INNIS, 446 U.S. 291 (1980)

RHODE ISLAND v. INNIS
446 U.S. 291 (1980)

FACTS: Police arrested Innis for the abduction and killing of a taxicab driver. The officer advised Innis of his *Miranda* rights and did not converse with him. When a sergeant and captain arrived at the scene, Innis was again advised of his *Miranda* rights. He replied that he understood his rights and wanted to speak to an attorney. Innis was placed in a police car to be transported to the police station. En route, two of the officers engaged in a conversation between themselves concerning Innis's shotgun, which had not been recovered. When one of the officers expressed concern that children from a nearby school for the handicapped might find the weapon and hurt themselves, Innis interrupted the conversation, saying that the officers should return to the scene so that he could show them where the shotgun was hidden. Upon returning to the scene, Innis was again advised of his *Miranda* rights. He again stated that he understood his rights but wanted to remove the gun before one of the children found it. He then led the police to the shotgun. Innis was charged with and convicted of robbery, kidnapping, and murder.

ISSUE: Did the conversation between the two police officers which prompted Innis to lead them to the shotgun constitute a custodial interrogation in the absence of his lawyer? NO.

SUPREME COURT DECISION: "Interrogation" refers not only to express questioning, but also the "functional equivalent" of questioning which involves any words or actions by the police which they should know are reasonably likely to elicit an incriminating response. In this instance, no such interrogation occurred, the conversation was merely a dialogue between two police officers; therefore, the evidence obtained by the police is admissible.

REASON: "Here there was no express questioning of respondent; the conversation between the two officers was, at least in form, nothing more than a dialogue between them to which no response from respondent was invited. Moreover, respondent was not subjected to the 'functional equivalent' of questioning since it cannot be said that the officers should have known that their conversation was reasonably likely to elicit an incriminating response from respondent. There is nothing in the record to suggest that the officers were aware that respondent was peculiarly susceptible to an appeal to his conscience concerning the safety of handicapped children, or that the police knew that respondent was unusually disoriented or upset at the time of his arrest. Nor does the record indicate that, in the context of a brief conversation, the officers should have known that respondent would suddenly be moved to make a self-incriminating response."

CASE SIGNIFICANCE: The *Miranda* case says that the *Miranda* warnings must be given whenever a suspect is subjected to "custodial interrogation." Subsequent cases have held that there is interrogation not only if questions are asked of a suspect, but also if police behavior amounts to the "functional equivalent" of actual questioning. An example is *Brewer v. Williams*, 430 U.S. 387 (1977) where the police officers, knowing the defendant's religious interest, made remarks designed to appeal to that interest and thus induced a confession even without directly asking the suspect questions. What the police did in this case, however, was not the "functional equivalent" of interrogation. As the Court said, "the conversation between the two officers was, at least in form, nothing more than a dialogue between them to which no response from respondent was invited." It is important for police officers to know that "interrogation" does not necessarily mean asking questions of the suspect. There are situations when the behavior of the police constitutes the "functional equivalent" of an interrogation (as in *Brewer*), but that was not the case here.

RELATED CASES:
CALIFORNIA v. BYERS, 402 U.S. 424 (1971)
MIRANDA v. ARIZONA, 384 U.S. 436 (1966)
NEW YORK v. QUARLES, 467 U.S. 649 (1984)
NIX v. WILLIAMS, 467 U.S. 431 (1984)

ARIZONA v. MAURO
481 U.S. 520 (1987)

FACTS: The police received a call that a man had just entered a store claiming that he had killed his son. When officers reached the store, Mauro admitted to committing the act and directed officers to the body. He was then arrested and advised of his rights under *Miranda v. Arizona*, 384 U.S. 436 (1966). He was taken to the police station where he again was given the *Miranda* warnings. Mauro told officers that he did not wish to make any more statements until a lawyer was present. At that time all questioning ceased. Following questioning in another room, Mauro's wife insisted on speaking with him. Police allowed the meeting on the condition that an officer be present and tape the conversation. The tape was used to impeach Mauro's contention that he was insane at the time of the murder. Mauro was charged with and convicted of murder and child abuse.

ISSUE: Does a conversation between a suspect and a spouse which is recorded by an officer constitute an interrogation under *Miranda v. Arizona*? NO.

SUPREME COURT DECISION: A conversation between a suspect and a spouse, which is recorded in the presence of an officer, does not constitute the functional equivalent of an interrogation under *Miranda v. Arizona*, 384 U.S. 436 (1966) and *Rhode Island v. Innis*, 446 U.S. 291 (1980). Evidence obtained during the conversation is, therefore, admissible in court.

REASON: "The purpose of *Miranda*...is to prevent the government from using the coercive nature of confinement to extract confessions that would not be given in an unrestrained environment. This purpose is not implicated here, since respondent was not subjected to compelling influences, psychological ploys, or direct questioning. There is no evidence that the police allowed the wife to meet with respondent in order to obtain incriminating statements. Moreover, police testimony, which the trial court found credible, indicated a number of legitimate reasons for an officer's presence at the meeting, including the wife's safety and various security considerations. Furthermore, an examination of the situation from respondent's perspective demonstrated the improbability that he would have felt he was being coerced to incriminate himself simply because he was told his wife would be allowed to speak to him."

CASE SIGNIFICANCE: This case defines the term "interrogation" as used in *Miranda*. In an earlier case (*Rhode Island v. Innis*, 446 U.S. 291 [1980]), the Court said that "interrogation" does not have to mean the actual asking of questions by the police; rather, it includes instances that amount to the "functional equivalent" of interrogation, meaning "words or actions by the police which they know are reasonably likely to elicit an incriminating response." The term "functional equivalent" is subjective and difficult to determine. Whatever its meaning may be, what the police did in this case (allowing the wife to talk with the husband and recording the conversation) was not the "functional equivalent" of an interrogation, hence, anything the suspect said during that conversation could be used against him in court. The police here merely "arranged a situation" wherein there was likelihood that the suspect would say something incriminating.

RELATED CASES:
EDWARDS v. ARIZONA, 451 U.S. 477 (1981)
MIRANDA v. ARIZONA, 384 U.S. 436 (1966)
NIX v. WILLIAMS, 467 U.S. 431 (1984)
RHODE ISLAND v. INNIS, 446 U.S. 291 (1980)

RIGHT TO COUNSEL 17

POWELL v. ALABAMA
287 U.S. 45 (1932)

FACTS: Nine black youths were charged with the rape of two white girls while on a train in Alabama. All were illiterate. The atmosphere in the town was such that the boys had to be held in a different town under military guard during the proceedings. The judge appointed "all members of the bar" to assist the boys during the proceedings; however, they were not represented by any attorney by name until the day of the trial. Each of the trials lasted only a day and resulted in a conviction. The youths were given the death penalty.

ISSUE: Were the accused in this case denied their constitutional rights to counsel and due process? YES.

SUPREME COURT DECISION: "In a capital case, where the defendant is unable to employ counsel, and is incapable adequately of making his own defense because of ignorance, feeblemindedness, illiteracy, or the like, it is the duty of the court, whether requested or not, to assign counsel for him as a necessary requisite of due process of law; and that duty is not discharged by an assignment at such a time or under such circumstances as to preclude the giving of effective aid in the preparation and trial of the case."

REASON: "Even the intelligent and educated layman has small and sometimes no skill in the science of the law. Left without aid of counsel, he may be put on trial without proper charge, and convicted upon incompetent evidence irrelevant to the issue or otherwise inadmissible against him. Without counsel, though he may not be guilty, he faces the danger of conviction because he does not know how to establish his innocence."

CASE SIGNIFICANCE: The Sixth Amendment to the Constitution provides that "in all criminal prosecutions, the accused shall enjoy the right...to have the assistance of counsel for his defence." This case provides the often-quoted reason, (quoted above and penned by Justice Sutherland), for this constitutional provision. Without a lawyer, an accused may be convicted, not because he or she is guilty, but because "he does not know how to establish his innocence." The right to counsel is a basic and fundamental right under the Constitution and must be respected by the police. Note that, in this case, the Court used the due process clause of the Fourteenth Amendment instead of the Sixth Amendment right to counsel to overturn the convictions. This is because, in 1932 when the case was decided, the provisions of the Bill of

Rights had not yet been extended to state proceedings. Were this case to be decided today, the Sixth Amendment right to counsel would have been used.

RELATED CASES:
ARGERSINGER v. HAMLIN, 407 U.S. 25 (1972)
BREWER v. WILLIAMS, 430 U.S. 387 (1977)
GIDEON v. WAINWRIGHT, 372 U.S. 335 (1963)
JOHNSON v. ZERBST, 304 U.S. 458 (1938)

GIDEON v. WAINWRIGHT
372 U.S. 335 (1963)

FACTS: Gideon was charged in a Florida state court with breaking and entering a poolroom with intent to commit a misdemeanor, an act classified as a felony offense under Florida law. Appearing in court without funds and without a lawyer, Gideon asked the court to appoint a lawyer for him. The court refused, saying that under Florida law the only time the court could appoint a lawyer to represent an accused was when the crime charged was a capital offense. Gideon conducted his own defense and was convicted.

ISSUE: Does the Constitution require the appointment of a lawyer for an indigent person who is charged in a state court with a felony offense? YES.

SUPREME COURT DECISION: The Sixth Amendment requires that a person charged with a felony offense in a state court must be given appointed counsel if he or she cannot afford one.

REASON: "The right of one charged with crime to counsel may not be deemed fundamental and essential to fair trials in some countries, but it is in ours. From the very beginning, our state and national constitutions and laws have laid great emphasis on procedural and substantive safeguards designed to assure fair trials before impartial tribunals in which every defendant stands equal before the law. This noble ideal cannot be realized if the poor man charged with a crime has to face his accusers without a lawyer to assist him..."

CASE SIGNIFICANCE: This case mandates that when an indigent is charged with a felony in a state court, counsel must be provided. This settled a controversy among lower courts which had inconsistent rulings on the type of offense an indigent had to be charged with in order to be entitled to a lawyer. An earlier case (*Betts v. Brady*, 316 U.S. 455, 1942), held that the requirement that counsel must be provided to all indigent defendants in federal felony trials did not extend to the states. This was overruled in the *Gideon* case when the Court held that the rule applied to criminal proceedings in state courts as well. Since 1963, both federal and state felony defendants must be given court appointed counsel if indigent. Note that the *Gideon* case required the appointment of counsel for indigents only in felony cases. This was later extended to misdemeanor cases in *Argersinger v. Hamlin* (see case in this book). Although not a case directly involving the police, the *Gideon* case is included here because it is helpful for the police to know what types of indigent offenders are entitled to a court-appointed lawyer during trial.

RELATED CASES:
ARGERSINGER v. HAMLIN, 407 U.S. 25 (1972)
BETTS v. BRADY, 316 U.S. 455 (1942)
MASSIAH v. UNITED STATES, 377 U.S. 201 (1964)
POWELL v. ALABAMA, 287 U.S. 45 (1932)

ESCOBEDO v. ILLINOIS
378 U.S. 478 (1964)

FACTS: Escobedo was arrested without a warrant and interrogated in connection with a murder. En route to the police station, officers told Escobedo that he had been named as the murderer and that he should admit to the crime. Escobedo replied that he wished to speak to an attorney. Shortly after Escobedo arrived at the police station, his retained lawyer arrived and asked permission from various police officials to speak with his client. His request was repeatedly denied. Escobedo also requested several times during an interrogation to speak to his attorney and was told that the attorney did not want to see him. Escobedo subsequently admitted to some knowledge of the murder and implicated himself as the murderer. Escobedo was charged with and convicted of murder.

ISSUE: Is a suspect entitled to a lawyer, if he or she requests one, during interrogation at a police station? YES.

SUPREME COURT DECISION: A suspect is entitled to a lawyer during interrogation at a police station. Denial of counsel in this case was a violation of the suspect's constitutional right to counsel because the investigation had focused on the suspect, he had been taken into custody, and he had requested and been denied an opportunity to consult with his lawyer.

REASON: "We hold, therefore, that, where, as here, the investigation is no longer a general inquiry into unsolved crime but has begun to focus on a particular suspect, the suspect has been taken into police custody, the police carry out a process of interrogations that lends itself to eliciting incriminating statements, the suspect has requested and been denied an opportunity to consult with his lawyer, and the police have not effectively warned him of his absolute right to remain silent, the accused has been denied 'the Assistance of Counsel' in violation of the Sixth amendment to the Constitution as 'made obligatory upon the States by the Fourteenth Amendment,' and that no statement elicited by the police during the interrogation may be used against him at a criminal trial."

CASE SIGNIFICANCE: This was an easy case for the Court to decide because the police had, indeed, grossly violated Escobedo's right to counsel. *Escobedo*, however, left two issues unsettled:

(1) Was the right to counsel available only when the suspect was accused of a serious offense, was being questioned at the police station, and had asked to see his lawyer? and,

(2) What did the Court mean when it said in the decision that the right to counsel could be invoked when the investigation had "begun to focus" on a particular suspect?

Because of its peculiar facts, the *Escobedo* case raised more questions than it answered. Lower court decisions disagreed on the meaning of *Escobedo*, leading to conflicting interpretations. Further guidance from the Supreme Court was necessary which led to the decision in *Miranda v. Arizona* (see case in this book). Because of the *Miranda* decision, the impact of *Escobedo* has been lessened because *Escobedo* only brought the right to counsel to the police station, whereas *Miranda* took it out into the streets.

RELATED CASES:
BREWER v. WILLIAMS, 430 U.S. 387 (1977)
EDWARDS v. ARIZONA, 451 U.S. 477 (1981)
MIRANDA v. ARIZONA, 384 U.S. 436 (1966)
WATTS v. INDIANA, 338 U.S. 49 (1949)

ARGERSINGER v. HAMLIN
407 U.S. 25 (1972)

FACTS: Argersinger, an indigent, was accused in a Florida court of carrying a concealed weapon, which was punishable by imprisonment of up to six months, a $1,000 fine, or both. He was tried before a judge but was not represented by a lawyer. He was convicted and sentenced to 90 days in jail.

ISSUE: Is an indigent defendant who is accused of a crime punishable by imprisonment of up to six months entitled to a court-appointed counsel during trial? YES.

SUPREME COURT DECISION: The right to counsel applies even in misdemeanor cases if the accused faces the possibility of imprisonment, however short that imprisonment may be.

REASON: "While there is historical support for limiting the 'deep commitment' to trial by jury to 'serious criminal cases,' there is no such support for a similar limitation on the right to assistance of counsel...."

"The Sixth Amendment thus extended the right to counsel beyond its common-law dimensions. But there is nothing in the language of the Amendment, its history, or in the decisions of this Court, to indicate that it was intended to embody a retraction of the right in petty offenses wherein the common law previously did require that counsel be provided....."

"We reject, therefore, the premise that since prosecutions for crimes punishable by imprisonment of less than six months may be tried without a jury, they may also be tried without a lawyer."

CASE SIGNIFICANCE: An earlier case, *Gideon v. Wainwright*, 372 U.S. 335 (1963), held that the right to counsel applies every time an accused is charged with a felony offense. The *Argersinger* case ruled that the right to counsel also applies to misdemeanor cases. The determining factor is whether the accused faces any possible jail or prison time under the law with which the defendant is charged. It does not matter that the accused is not, in fact, sent to prison or jail after conviction. What matters is that the offense charged carried a *possible* jail or prison term. *Argersinger* is not a police case, but it embodies current case law on what offenses entitle an indigent defendant to a lawyer during trial. This is knowledge that is helpful to law enforcement officers.

RELATED CASES:
GIDEON v. WAINWRIGHT, 372 U.S. 335 (1963)
MASSIAH v. UNITED STATES, 377 U.S. 201 (1964)
POWELL v. ALABAMA, 287 U.S. 45 (1932)
WASHINGTON v. TEXAS, 388 U.S. 14 (1967)

UNITED STATES v. HENRY
447 U.S. 264 (1980)

FACTS: Henry was indicted for armed robbery and incarcerated. While in jail, government agents contacted an informant who was a cell mate of Henry and instructed him to be alert to any statements made by Henry but not to initiate any conversations regarding the robbery. After the informant had been released from jail, he was contacted by the agents and paid for information he provided them concerning incriminating statements Henry made to him in reference to the robbery. There was no indication that the informant would have been paid had he not provided such information. Henry was convicted of bank robbery, partly on the testimony of the informant.

ISSUE: Is a defendant denied the right to counsel under the Sixth Amendment if the government uses a paid informant to create a situation likely to induce incriminating statements? YES.

SUPREME COURT DECISION: The government violates a defendant's Sixth Amendment right to counsel by intentionally creating a situation likely to elicit incriminating statements.

REASON: "The question here is whether under the facts of this case a Government agent 'deliberately elicited' incriminating statements from Henry.... Three factors are important. First, Nichols [the informant] was acting under instructions as a paid informant for the Government; second, Nichols was ostensibly no more than a fellow inmate of Henry; and third, Henry was in custody under indictment at the time he was engaged in conversation with Nichols."

"The Government argues that federal agents instructed Nichols not to question Henry about the robbery. Yet according to his own testimony, Nichols was not a passive listener; rather, he had 'some conversations with Mr. Henry' while he was in jail and Henry's incriminatory statements were 'the product of this conversation.'"

CASE SIGNIFICANCE: This is a right-to-counsel rather than a self-incrimination case. The evidence obtained was excluded because what the government did violated the suspect's right to a lawyer, not because what the government did amounted to a form of interrogation. The Court said that, here, the government created a situation likely to induce the suspect to make incriminating statements without the assistance of counsel. Some observers find it difficult to accept this logic particularly because the informant was instructed to simply listen to incriminating statements Henry made and not to interrogate him at all. Nonetheless, the Court said that incriminating statements were "deliberately elicited" by the informant, which the police cannot do in the absence of a lawyer. Great weight was given by the Court to the fact that the informant was acting under government instruction and that Henry was in custody under indictment at the time the incriminating statements were made. Moreover, the informant in fact engaged Henry in conversations which produced the incriminating statements.

This case was not decided under *Miranda v. Arizona*, 384 U.S. 436 (1966), but under *Massiah v. United States*, 377 U.S. 201 (1964). In *Massiah*, the Court said that when a police informer carries into a suspect's home an electronic device that transmits the conversation to the police outside, the evidence is not admissible if the defendant was questioned without a lawyer after one had been retained. The police ought to be careful when interviewing or interrogating an accused or a suspect who has retained a lawyer. In these cases, courts frown upon such interrogations, not because no *Miranda* warnings were given, but because a suspect's counsel has a right to be present whenever his or her client is questioned by the police.

RELATED CASES:
MASSIAH v. UNITED STATES, 377 U.S. 201 (1964)
RHODE ISLAND v. INNIS, 446 U.S. 291 (1980)
SPANO v. NEW YORK, 360 U.S. 315 (1959)
UNITED STATES v. ASH, 413 U.S. 300 (1973)

MASSIAH v. UNITED STATES
377 U.S. 201 (1964)

FACTS: Customs officials received information that Massiah was transporting narcotics from South America aboard a ship on which he was a merchant seaman. Officials searched the ship and found 300 pounds of cocaine. Massiah was indicted for possession of narcotics aboard a United States vessel. While out on bail, officials enlisted the aid of one of Massiah's confederates. The confederate allowed officials to install a transmitter under the front seat of his automobile, then engaged Massiah in a conversation which could be overheard by officials. These incriminating statements were admitted over Massiah's objection at trial and he was convicted.

ISSUE: Are statements obtained through electronic eavesdropping and the use of an informant, which are elicited after the filing of formal charges and in the absence of the suspect, a violation of the Sixth Amendment's right to counsel? YES.

SUPREME COURT DECISION: Evidence in the form of incriminating statements is not admissible in court if the defendant was questioned without an attorney by police agents after the defendant has been charged and has obtained a lawyer. The evidence is inadmissible, not because there was a violation of the right against unreasonable search and seizure but because the right to counsel under the Sixth Amendment has been violated.

REASON: "We hold that the petitioner was denied the basic protections of the guarantee [of the Sixth Amendment] when there was used against him at his trial evidence of his own incriminating words, which federal agents had deliberately elicited from him after he had been indicted and in the absence of his counsel. It is true that in *Spano* [*v. New York*, 360 U.S. 315 (1959)] the defendant was interrogated in a police station while here the damaging testimony was elicited from the defendant without his knowledge while he was free on bail. But, as Judge Hays pointed out in his dissent in the Court of Appeals, 'if such a rule is to have any efficacy it must apply to indirect and surreptitious interrogations as well as those conducted in the jailhouse. In this case, Massiah was more seriously imposed upon...because he did not even know that he was under interrogation by a government agent."

CASE SIGNIFICANCE: This case, although involving electronic surveillance, is really a right-to-counsel case. The Court discussed the electronic surveillance issue only briefly. It reserved most of its discussion to the right to counsel issue, concluding that, while evidence was obtained validly with the use of radio equipment, it had to be excluded because the suspect's right to counsel was violated. It is important to note that here the suspect had been formally charged in court and had obtained an attorney. If these factors had not been present, the evidence would have been admissible.

RELATED CASES:
ESCOBEDO v. ILLINOIS, 378 U.S. 478 (1964)
HOFFA v. UNITED STATES, 385 U.S. 293 (1966)
SPANO v. NEW YORK, 360 U.S. 315 (1959)
UNITED STATES v. HENRY, 447 U.S. 264 (1980)

ENTRAPMENT 18

SHERMAN v. UNITED STATES
356 U.S. 369 (1958)

FACTS: A government informant met Sherman in a doctor's office where both were being treated for drug addiction. On several subsequent chance meetings, the informant asked Sherman if he knew a source of drugs. Sherman avoided the issue, but after several requests, Sherman offered to supply narcotics. Several times thereafter, Sherman supplied the informant with drugs for cost plus expenses. The informant notified FBI agents of the transactions and set up narcotics deals on three more occasions, which agents observed. Sherman was arrested, tried, and convicted of drug offenses.

ISSUE: Were the actions of the government informant such that they induced Sherman to commit the crimes he would have otherwise been unwilling to commit, resulting in entrapment? YES.

SUPREME COURT DECISION: There is entrapment when the government induces an individual to commit a crime which he or she otherwise would not have attempted.

REASON: "The case at bar illustrates an evil which the defense of entrapment is designed to overcome. The government informer entices someone attempting to avoid narcotics not only into carrying out an illegal sale but also returning to the habit of use. Selecting the proper time, the informer then tells the government agent. The setup is accepted by the agent without even a question as to the manner in which the informer encountered the seller. Thus the government plays on the weakness of an innocent party and beguiles him into committing crimes which he otherwise would not have attempted. Law enforcement does not require methods such as this."

CASE SIGNIFICANCE: This case sets the current test used by many courts for entrapment, namely: there is entrapment if the government induces an individual to commit a crime which he or she otherwise would not have committed. In this case, the informant asked Sherman if he knew a drug supplier and then whether Sherman himself would provide the narcotics. Sherman first avoided the issue, but then gave in after repeated requests. It is clear that, in this case, Sherman would not have committed the crime had the government officials, in effect, not forced him to do so. This case also decided that the accused bears the burden of proving entrapment and that the factual issue of whether or not the defendant was actually entrapped is a question of fact, not a question of law, and is, therefore, for the jury to decide.

RELATED CASES:
HAMPTON v. UNITED STATES, 425 U.S. 484 (1976)
MATHEWS v. UNITED STATES, 108 S. Ct. 883 (1988)
RUSSELL v. UNITED STATES, 411 U.S. 423 (1973)
SORRELS v UNITED STATES, 287 U.S. 435 (1932)

UNITED STATES v. RUSSELL
411 U.S. 423 (1973)

FACTS: Russell and two others were indicted and convicted of illegally manufacturing and selling methamphetamine, a prohibited drug. Shapiro, an agent of the Federal Bureau of Narcotics and Dangerous Drugs, had met earlier with the three accused and told them that he represented a group desiring to obtain control of the manufacture and distribution of the drug. Shapiro offered to supply them with phenyl-2-propanone, a chemical required to manufacture methamphetamine. In return, Shapiro wanted to receive one-half of the speed made with the ingredient supplied. Shapiro later received his share and also bought some of the remainder from Russell. There was testimony at the trial that phenyl-2-propanone was generally difficult to obtain because, at the request of the Bureau of Narcotics and Dangerous Drugs, some chemical supply firms had voluntarily ceased to sell the chemical. On appeal Russell conceded that the jury could have found him predisposed to commit the offenses with which he was charged, but argued that he was entrapped as a matter of law.

ISSUE: Did the act by the undercover government agent of providing an essential chemical for the manufacture of a prohibited drug constitute entrapment? NO.

SUPREME COURT DECISION: The act by a government agent of supplying one of the necessary ingredients for the manufacture of a prohibited drug does not constitute entrapment. That conduct stops short of being a violation of "fundamental fairness" that would shock "the universal sense of justice." This is a case of an accused who was an "unwary criminal" and not an "unwary innocent," for whom the entrapment defense would have been available.

REASON: "While we may some day be presented with a situation in which the conduct of law enforcement agents is so outrageous that due process principles would absolutely bar the government from invoking judicial processes to obtain conviction, the instant case is distinctly not of that breed. Shapiro's contribution of propanone to the criminal enterprise already in process was scarcely objectionable. The chemical is by itself a harmless substance and its possession is legal. While the government may have been seeking to make it more difficult for drug rings, such as that of which respondent was a member, to obtain the chemical, the evidence described above shows that it nonetheless was obtainable. The law enforcement conduct here stops short of violating that 'fundamental fairness, shocking to the universal sense of justice,' mandated by the Due Process Clause of the Fifth Amendment."

CASE SIGNIFICANCE: The *Russell* case illustrates the majority view on the entrapment defense. This view focuses on the predisposition of the defendant to commit the alleged act rather than on an analysis of the conduct of the government. Under this view, the entrapment defense applies only if the accused has no predisposition to commit the crime, but does so because of inducement by a government agent. The Court minimized the importance of Shapiro's supplying the accused with an essential ingredient for the manufacture of the prohibited drug, saying that the chemical was a harmless substance and its possession was legal. Besides, although it was difficult to obtain the chemical, the evidence showed that it was, nonetheless, obtainable; therefore, the conduct of the government agent stopped short of violating the "fundamental fairness" mandated by the Due Process Cause of the Fifth Amendment. In using this language, the Court strongly implies that, even under the majority test, there may be conduct by the government that may entrap a person who is predisposed to commit a crime. The Court, however, did not give any example of that type of prohibited government conduct. Note that, had the Court here used the minority (objective) test, the accused most probably would have been acquitted.

RELATED CASES:
HAMPTON v. UNITED STATES, 425 U.S. 484 (1976)
MATHEWS v. UNITED STATES, 108 S. Ct. 833 (1988)
SHERMAN v. UNITED STATES, 356 U.S. 369 (1958)
SORRELS v. UNITED STATES, 287 U.S. 435 (1932)

HAMPTON v. UNITED STATES
425 U.S. 484 (1976)

FACTS: Hampton was convicted of two counts of distributing heroin in violation of federal law. The conviction arose from two sales of heroin by Hampton to agents of the Drug Enforcement Administration. The sales were arranged by an acquaintance of Hampton who was also a DEA informant. Hampton claimed entrapment, stating that he neither intended to sell, nor knew that he was dealing in heroin and that all of the drugs he sold were supplied by the acquaintance who was also a government informant.

ISSUE: Is there entrapment when a government informant supplies heroin to a suspect, who then sells it to government agents? NO.

SUPREME COURT DECISION: There was no entrapment here because the government informant supplied heroin to a suspect who had the predisposition to commit the crime. The entrapment defense applies only if the accused had no predisposition to commit the crime but was induced to do so by government agents.

REASON: "Here...the police, the government informant, and the defendant acted in concert with one another. If the result of the governmental activity is to 'implant in the mind of an innocent person the disposition to commit the alleged offense and induce its commission,' the defendant is protected by the defense of entrapment. If the police engaged in illegal activity in concert with a defendant beyond the scope of their duties, the remedy lies not in freeing the equally culpable defendant but in the prosecuting the police under the applicable provisions of state or federal law."

CASE SIGNIFICANCE: To civil libertarians, this decision is shocking, that there is no entrapment even when a government informant supplies an illegal substance to an accused who then sells it to government agents. This case expanded the ruling in *Russell* (see brief in this book). In the *Russell* case, the government informant provided the defendant with a difficult-to-obtain but legal item. In this case, however, the item provided was heroin, an illegal drug.

There are two views on the entrapment defense. The *Hampton* case reiterates the majority view which focuses on the conduct of the defendant, rather than on the conduct of the government agents. Under this test, if the defendant is predisposed to commit the crime, there is no entrapment, regardless of the conduct of the government agents. Using this test, there was no entrapment in this case although the conduct of the government informant in providing the accused with heroin was extreme, if not gross. In contrast, the minority view rejects the predisposition test and focuses solely on the conduct of the government. If the conduct of the government is outrageous, the accused is entitled to the entrapment defense even if he or she is predisposed to commit the crime. Under this minority view, Hampton could have successfully claimed entrapment because the conduct of the government was indeed outrageous. The Court, however, rejected this view (as it did in the *Russell* case) and took into account Hampton's predisposition. The current majority view on entrapment is: if a suspect is predisposed to commit the crime, there is no entrapment, regardless of the conduct of the government. Note, however, that state law or court decisions determine the entrapment rule in a particular state; the *Hampton* rule only applies in federal cases. State entrapment defenses depend on whether a state uses the majority or minority view. Police officers must be familiar with state law on the entrapment defense.

RELATED CASES:
MATHEWS v. UNITED STATES, 485 U.S. 58 (1988)
RUSSELL v. UNITED STATES, 411 U.S. 423 (1973)
SHERMAN v. UNITED STATES, 356 U.S. 369 (1958)
SORRELS v UNITED STATES, 287 U.S. 435 (1932)

MATHEWS v. UNITED STATES
485 U.S. 58 (1988)

FACTS: A government informant, under the surveillance of the FBI officers, requested a loan from Mathews in return for Small Business Association benefits. When the two met to exchange the money, Mathews was arrested for accepting a bribe in exchange for government services. The trial court denied Matthew's motion seeking to raise the affirmative defense of entrapment because he would not admit all the elements of the crime. Mathews was ultimately found guilty of accepting an unlawful gratuity.

ISSUE: Can a defendant in a federal criminal prosecution deny an element of a crime and still raise the entrapment defense? YES.

SUPREME COURT DECISION: Even if the defendant in a federal criminal case denies one or more elements of the crime, the affirmative defense of entrapment may be raised if there is sufficient evidence from which a reasonable jury could conclude that there was entrapment.

REASON: "Even if the defendant in a federal criminal case denies one or more elements of the crime, he is entitled to an entrapment instruction whenever there is sufficient evidence from which a reasonable jury could find entrapment....There is no merit to the Government's contention that, because entrapment presupposes the commission of a crime, defendant should not be allowed both to deny the offense or an element thereof, and to rely on the inconsistent, affirmative defense of entrapment."

CASE SIGNIFICANCE: The *Mathews* case resolves an issue that generated inconsistent decisions among the various federal courts of appeals. In previous cases, the Third, Sixth, and Seventh Circuits allowed the entrapment defense only if the defendant admitted to committing all the elements of the crime charged. By contrast, the Ninth and the District of Columbia Circuits allowed the raising of the entrapment defense even if the accused denied any or all elements of the offense charged. The Circuits that allowed the entrapment defense only if the defendant admitted to having committed all the element of the crime charged maintained that a defendant's denial of one of the elements was inconsistent with the entrapment defense, saying that there was no entrapment if one of the elements of the offense was not in fact committed. These same circuits reasoned that to allow a defendant to assert inconsistent defenses encouraged perjury and confused the court. The Courts in *Mathews* rejected these claims, saying that the issue was not whether defendant's claims were inconsistent, but whether sufficient evidence existed from which a reasonable jury could find entrapment. That is a question for the trial judge to decide.

RELATED CASES:
HAMPTON v. UNITED STATES, 425 U.S. 484 (1976)
RUSSELL v. UNITED STATES, 411 U.S. 423 (1973)
SHERMAN v. UNITED STATES, 356 U.S. 369 (1958)
SORRELS v. UNITED STATES, 287 U.S. 435 (1932)

LEGAL LIABILITIES 19

OMEN v. CITY OF INDEPENDENCE, MO, 445 U.S. 622 (1980)
HARLOW v. FITZGERALD, 457 U.S. 800 (1982)
BRISCOE v. LaHUE, 460 U.S. 325 (1983)
MALLEY v. BRIGGS, 475 U.S. 335 (1986)
CITY OF CANTON v. HARRIS, 109 S. Ct. 1197 (1989)
WILL v. MICHIGAN, 109 S. Ct. 2304 (1989)

OWEN v. CITY OF INDEPENDENCE, MO.
445 U.S. 622 (1980)

FACTS: The City Council of Independence, Missouri, decided that reports of an investigation of the police department be released to the news media and turned over to the prosecutor for presentation to the grand jury and that the city manager take appropriate action against the persons involved in the wrongful activities. Acting on this, the city manager dismissed the chief of police. No reason was given for the dismissal. The chief of police received only a written notice stating that the dismissal was made in accordance with a specified provision of the city charter. The chief of police filed a 42 U.S.C. §1983 lawsuit against the city manager and members of the city council, alleging that he was discharged without notice of reasons and without a hearing, thereby violating his constitutional rights to procedural and substantive due process. The District Court decided for the city manager and council members.

ISSUE: Are municipalities and municipal officials entitled to the "good faith" defense if a right is violated while officials are following the provisions of a city policy or custom? NO.

SUPREME COURT DECISION: A municipality has no immunity to liability under § 1983 flowing from violations of an individual's constitutional rights and may not assert the "good faith" defense that is available to its officers.

REASON: "We believe that today's decision, together with prior precedents in this area, properly allocates these costs among the three principals in the scenario of the Section 1983 cause of action: the victim of the constitutional deprivation; the officer whose conduct caused the injury; and the public, as represented by the municipal entity. The innocent individual who is harmed by an abuse of governmental authority is assured that he will be compensated for his injury. The offending official, so long as he conducts himself in good faith may go about his business secure in the knowledge that a qualified immunity will protect him from personal liability for damages that are more appropriately chargeable to the populace as a whole. And the public will be forced to bear only the costs of injury inflicted by the 'execution of a government's policy or custom, whether made by its lawmakers or by those whose edicts or acts may fairly be said to represent official policy.'"

CASE SIGNIFICANCE: The *Owen* case makes clear that the municipality may be liable if a person's constitutional right is violated (in this case the right to due process prior to dismissal) by public officials who are acting in accordance with agency policy as contained in the city charter. Because they were acting in accordance with the provisions of the city charter, the city manager and members of the city counsel enjoyed a "good faith" defense, but the city did not. The implication is that municipalities must make sure that their policy does not violate individual rights. The fact that something is official policy does not mean that it is automatically valid. The Court said that individual blameworthiness is no longer the acid test of liability, substituting in its place the principle of "equitable loss-spreading," in addition to fault, as a fact in distributing the costs of official misconduct.

RELATED CASES:
WISCONSIN v. CONSTANTINEAU, 400 U.S. 433 (1971)
IMBLER v. PACTMAN, 424 U.S. 409 (1976)
MONELL v. NEW YORK CITY DEPARTMENT
    OF SOCIAL SERVICES, 436 U.S. 658 (1978)
SCHEUER v. RHODES, 416 U.S. 232 (1974)

HARLOW v. FITZGERALD
457 U.S. 800 (1982)

FACTS: Harlow and Butterfield, senior aides of President Nixon, were accused of violating Fitzgerald's constitutional rights by conspiring to have Fitzgerald dismissed as an Air Force official. Fitzgerald's allegations against Harlow stemmed from several conversations in which Harlow discussed Fitzgerald's dismissal with the Air Force Secretary. Allegations against Butterfield were based on a memorandum circulated by Butterfield in which he claimed that Fitzgerald planned to "blow the whistle" on Air Force purchasing practices. Fitzgerald alleged that his dismissal was in retaliation of these actions. Fitzgerald filed a lawsuit for unlawful discharge.

ISSUE: Do government officials have absolute immunity when performing discretionary official functions of their jobs, such as dismissing a subordinate? NO.

SUPREME COURT DECISION: Government officials performing discretionary functions are not guaranteed absolute immunity but instead enjoy only qualified immunity. This means that they are shielded from liability for civil damages only "if their conduct does not violate clearly established statutory or constitutional rights of which a reasonable person would have known."

REASON: "Reliance on the objective reasonableness of an official's conduct, as measured by reference to clearly established law, should avoid excessive disruption of government....On summary judgement, the judge appropriately may determine, not only the applicable law, but whether that law was clearly established at the time an action occurred. If the law at that time was not clearly established, an official could not reasonably be expected to anticipate subsequent legal developments, nor could he fairly be said to 'know' that the law forbade conduct not previously identified as unlawful....If the law was clearly established, the immunity defense ordinarily should fail, since a reasonably competent public official should know the law governing his conduct. Nevertheless, if the official pleading the defense claims extraordinary circumstances and can prove that he neither knew nor should have known the relevant legal standard, the defense should be sustained...."

CASE SIGNIFICANCE: This case involved officials in the office of the United States President, not the police. The principle, however, applies to all public officials. The *Fitzgerald* case is important because it set a new test for the "good faith" defense available to public officials. The old test (enunciated by the Court in *Wood v. Strickland*, 420 U.S. 308 [1975]) was that a government official asserting the defense "took action with the malicious intention to cause deprivation of constitutional rights or other injury." The new test, under *Fitzgerald*, is that public officials are not civilly liable "if their conduct does not violate clearly established statutory or constitutional rights of which a reasonable person would have known." This new test has a "good new and bad news" side to it. The "good news" is that not every violation of a constitutional right by a police officer leads to civil liability. There is civil liability only if the officer violated a "clearly established statutory or constitutional rights of which a reasonable person would have known." The "bad news" is that police officers have an obligation to know the clearly established rights of the public. This requires a good working knowledge of criminal procedure and constitutional law.

RELATED CASES:
BUTZ v. ECONOMOU, 438 U.S. 478
GRAVEL v. UNITED STATES, 408 U.S. 606 (1972)

NIXON v. FITZGERALD, 457 U.S. 731 (1981)
SCHEUER v. RHODES, 416 U.S. 232 (1974)

BRISCOE v. LaHUE
460 U.S. 325 (1983)

FACTS: Briscoe was convicted in a state court of burglary. He then filed a 42 U.S.C. Section 1983 suit in the District Court alleging that LaHue, a police officer, had violated his right to due process by committing perjury in the criminal proceeding leading to his conviction.

ISSUE: May a police officer be liable in a Section 1983 case for giving perjured testimony? NO.

SUPREME COURT DECISION: Police officers enjoy absolute immunity from civil liability when testifying, even if the testimony is perjured.

REASON: "The common law provided absolute immunity from subsequent damages liability for all persons -- governmental or otherwise -- who are integral parts of the judicial process....When a police officer appears as a witness, he may reasonably be viewed as acting like any witness sworn to tell the truth, in which event he can make a strong claim to witness immunity. Alternatively, he may be regarded as an official performing a critical role in the judicial process, in which even he may seek the benefit afforded to other governmental participants in the same proceeding. Nothing in Section 1983 language suggests that a police officer witness belongs in a narrow, special category lacking protection against damages suits."

CASE SIGNIFICANCE: This decision assures police officers that they cannot be held liable under 42 U.S.C. § 1983 (the usual type of civil liability cases filed against government officials) for giving false testimony against a defendant in a criminal trial. The Court gives two reasons for this absolute immunity. First, the officer is just like any other witness who is sworn to tell the truth and, therefore, enjoys witness immunity. Second, the officer is a public official performing a critical role in the judicial process. The decision does not mean, however, that officers have complete freedom to tell falsehoods in court. The officer who does so may be held liable under the state penal code, usually for perjury. Note that, only when testifying in court, does an officer enjoy absolute immunity. In all other aspects of police work, an officer enjoys only qualified (good faith) immunity.

RELATED CASES:
CLARK v. HILLIARD, 423 U.S. 1066 (1976)
HARLOW v. FITZGERALD, 457 U.S. 800 (1982)
IMBLER v. PACTMAN, 424 U.S. 409 (1976)
PIERSON v. RAY, 386 U.S. 547 (1967)

MALLEY v. BRIGGS
475 U.S. 335 (1986)

FACTS: On the basis of two monitored telephone calls pursuant to a court-authorized wiretap, Rhode Island state trooper Malley prepared felony complaints charging Briggs and others with possession of marijuana. The complaints were given to a state judge together with arrest warrants and supporting affidavits. The judge signed the warrants, and the defendants were arrested. The charges, however, were subsequently dropped when the grand jury refused to return an indictment. The defendants then brought action under 42 U.S.C 1983, alleging that Malley, in applying for the arrest warrants, had violated their rights against unreasonable search and seizure.

ISSUE: Is absolute immunity accorded a defendant police officer in 42 U.S.C. § 1983 actions when it is alleged that the officer caused the plaintiffs to be unconstitutionally arrested by presenting a judge with a complaint and a supporting affidavit that failed to establish probable cause? NO.

SUPREME COURT DECISION: A police officer is not entitled to absolute immunity, but only qualified immunity to liability for damages in Section 1983 cases.

REASON: "Although we have previously held that police officers sued under Section 1983 for false arrest are qualifiedly immune, petitioner urges that he should be absolutely immune because his function in seeking an arrest warrant was similar to that of a complaining witness. The difficulty with this submission is that complaining witnesses were not absolutely immune at common law. In 1871, the generally accepted rule was that one who procured the issuance of an arrest warrant by submitting a complaint could be held liable if the complaint was made maliciously and without probable cause. Given malice and the lack of probable case, the complainant enjoyed no immunity. The common law thus affords no support for the petitioner."

CASE SIGNIFICANCE: Officer Malley argued that he be given absolute immunity because his function in seeking an arrest warrant was similar to that of a complaining witness. The Court said that complaining witnesses were not absolutely immune at common law. If malice and lack of probable cause are proved, the officer enjoys no absolute immunity. The Court also rejected the officer's argument that policy considerations require absolute immunity for the officer applying for a warrant, saying that, as the qualified immunity defense has evolved, it provides ample protection to all but the plainly incompetent or those who knowingly violated the law. The Court considered this protection sufficient because, under current standards, the officer is not liable anyway if he or she acted in an objectively reasonable manner. The *Malley* case, therefore, makes clear that under no circumstances, will the Court extend the "absolute immunity" defense (available to judges, prosecutors, and legislators) to police officers. The only exception is when the officer is testifying in a criminal trial. This means that officers enjoy only qualified immunity, but that they will not be liable if they act in an objectively reasonable manner.

RELATED CASES:
BUTZ v. ECONOMOU, 438 U.S. 478 (1978)
HARLOW v. FITZGERALD, 457 U.S. 800 (1982)
PIERSON v. RAY, 386 U.S. 547 (1967)
TOWER v. GLOVER, 467 U.S. 914 (1984)

CITY OF CANTON v. HARRIS
109 S. Ct. 1197 (1989)

FACTS: Harris was arrested and taken to the police stations in a patrol wagon. Upon arrival at the station, Harris was found sitting on the floor of the wagon. When asked if she needed medical help her reply was incoherent. Harris fell twice more during her stay at the station. She was ultimately left lying on the floor to prevent her from falling again. The officers did not offer medical assistance. When she was released an hour later, she was taken by an ambulance provided by her family to a hospital where she was diagnosed as having several emotional ailments and was hospitalized. Harris filed a 42

U.S.C. § 1983 lawsuit against the city for failure to provide her with adequate medical care while in police custody.

ISSUE: Can a municipality be held liable in a Section 1983 suit for constitutional violations resulting from a failure to properly train municipal employees? YES.

SUPREME COURT DECISION: Inadequate police training may serve as the basis for municipal liability under Section 1983, but only if the failure to train amounts to deliberate indifference to the rights of persons with whom the police come into contact and the deficiency in the training program is closely related to the injury suffered.

REASON: "Only where a failure to train reflects a 'deliberate' or 'conscious' choice by the municipality can the failure to be properly thought of as actionable city 'policy.'...[T]he focus must be on whether the program is adequate to the tasks the particular employees must perform, and if it is not, on whether such inadequate training can justifiably be said to represent 'city policy.' Moreover, the identified deficiency in the training program must be closely related to the ultimate injury. Thus, respondent still must prove that the deficiency in training actually caused the police officers' indifference to her medical needs. To adopt lesser standards of fault and causation would open municipalities to unprecedented liability under Section 1983; would result in *de facto respondeat superior* liability, a result rejected in *Monell*; would engage federal courts in an endless exercise of second-guessing municipal employee-training programs, a task that they are ill suited to undertake; and would implicate serious questions of federalism."

CASE SIGNIFICANCE: This case settles an issue that has long bothered lower courts: "can a municipality be held liable for failure to train?" The Court in this case answered yes, but subject to strict requirements. These requirements are:
  (1) the failure to adequately train reflects a "deliberate" or "conscious" choice by the municipality;
  (2) such inadequate training must represent city policy; and
  (3) the identified deficiency in the training program must be closely related to the ultimate injury.

What this means is that not every injury caused by police officers leads to municipal liability for failure to train. It is only when the three requirements above are met that municipal liability ensues. These three requirements are usually hard for plaintiffs in Section 1983 cases to establish, hence discouraging the "deep pockets" approach (where the municipality is involved in the lawsuit because of a greater ability to pay than the police officer) often used in civil rights liability cases. No liability on the part of the municipality for failure to train does not mean that the officer cannot be held liable. There are instances when an officer may be liable even if the municipality is not liable for failure to train.

RELATED CASES:
MONELL v. NEW YORK CITY DEPARTMENT OF SOCIAL SERVICES, 436 U.S. 658 (1978)
OKLAHOMA CITY v. TUTTLE, 471 U.S. 808 (1985)
PEMBAUR v. CINCINNATI, 475 U.S. 469 (1986)
SPRINGFIELD v. KIBBE, 480 U.S. 257 (1987)

WILL v. MICHIGAN DEPARTMENT OF STATE POLICE
109 S. Ct. 2304 (1989)

FACTS: Will filed a 42 U.S.C. § 1983 lawsuit alleging that he was denied a promotion, in violation of his constitutional rights, to a data systems analyst position in the department because his brother had been a student activist and the subject of a "red squad" file maintained by the department. He named as defendants the Michigan Department of State Police and the Director of the State Police in his official capacity.

ISSUE: May state officials, acting in their official capacity, be sued under Section 1983 in a state court? NO.

SUPREME COURT DECISION: Neither the State nor State officials acting in their official capacity may be sued under Section 1983 in a state court. A suit against State officials in their official capacity is a suit against the State itself and, therefore, will not succeed because a State cannot be sued under Section 1983.

REASON: "Section 1983 provides a federal forum to remedy many deprivations of civil liabilities. The Eleventh Amendment bars such suits unless the State has waived its immunity....Given that a principle purpose behind the enactment of Section 1983 was to provide a federal forum for civil rights claims, and that Congress did not provide such a federal forum for civil rights claims against States, we cannot accept petitioner's argument that Congress intended nevertheless to create a cause of action against States to be brought in State courts, which are precisely the courts Congress sought to allow civil rights claimants to avoid through Section 1983."

CASE SIGNIFICANCE: This decision has limited significance because it applies only to State law enforcement officials, not to the local police. Public officials can be sued either in their public or private capacity. If sued in their public capacity, the agency will most likely pay if the officer is held liable, as long as the officer acted within their scope of authority. If sued in their private capacity, liability is personal with the officer so the agency will most likely refuse to pay. Plaintiffs prefer to sue officials in their public (official) capacity because of the "deep pockets" theory. The *Will* case says that state officials cannot be sued under Section 1983 in their official capacity because the Eleventh Amendment exempts States from liability in such lawsuits, unless the liability is waived by the State. This decision extends State immunity to state public officials when sued in their official capacity on the grounds that such lawsuits are, in fact, lawsuits against the State. The following points need to be emphasized, however, in connection with this decision. These are:

(1) Although State officials cannot now be sued in their official capacity in a Section 1983 lawsuit, they can be sued in their personal capacity, although that approach is less attractive to plaintiffs;

(2) State officials can be sued in their official or personal capacity in a state tort case because the *Will* case only applies to Section 1983 cases; and

(3) The *Will* case applies only to State public officials. Most law enforcement officers are municipal or county officials and, therefore, may be sued in either their public or private capacity under Section 1983. This is because the Eleventh Amendment grants immunity to States, not to local government.

(4) State officials have immunity from Section 1983 cases in federal courts. The *Will* case says that they now have immunity in Section 1983 cases filed in state courts. The problem, however, is that many states have waived sovereign immunity and, therefore, expose state officials to possible liability.

RELATED CASES:
IMBLER v. PACTMAN, 424 U.S. 409 (1976)
MONELL v. DEPARTMENT OF SOCIAL SERVICES,
    436 U.S. 658 (1978)
OWEN v. CITY OF INDEPENDENCE, 445 U.S. 622 (1980)
SCHEUER v. RHODES, 416 U.S. 232 (1974)